C-3213   CAREER EXAMINATION SERIES

This is your
PASSBOOK for...

Infection Control Nurse

Test Preparation Study Guide
Questions & Answers

COPYRIGHT NOTICE

This book is SOLELY intended for, is sold ONLY to, and its use is RESTRICTED to individual, bona fide applicants or candidates who qualify by virtue of having seriously filed applications for appropriate license, certificate, professional and/or promotional advancement, higher school matriculation, scholarship, or other legitimate requirements of education and/or governmental authorities.

This book is NOT intended for use, class instruction, tutoring, training, duplication, copying, reprinting, excerption, or adaptation, etc., by:

1) Other publishers
2) Proprietors and/or Instructors of "Coaching" and/or Preparatory Courses
3) Personnel and/or Training Divisions of commercial, industrial, and governmental organizations
4) Schools, colleges, or universities and/or their departments and staffs, including teachers and other personnel
5) Testing Agencies or Bureaus
6) Study groups which seek by the purchase of a single volume to copy and/or duplicate and/or adapt this material for use by the group as a whole without having purchased individual volumes for each of the members of the group
7) Et al.

Such persons would be in violation of appropriate Federal and State statutes.

PROVISION OF LICENSING AGREEMENTS – Recognized educational, commercial, industrial, and governmental institutions and organizations, and others legitimately engaged in educational pursuits, including training, testing, and measurement activities, may address request for a licensing agreement to the copyright owners, who will determine whether, and under what conditions, including fees and charges, the materials in this book may be used them. In other words, a licensing facility exists for the legitimate use of the material in this book on other than an individual basis. However, it is asseverated and affirmed here that the material in this book CANNOT be used without the receipt of the express permission of such a licensing agreement from the Publishers. Inquiries re licensing should be addressed to the company, attention rights and permissions department.

All rights reserved, including the right of reproduction in whole or in part, in any form or by any means, electronic or mechanical, including photocopying, recording, or by any information storage and retrieval system, without permission in writing from the Publisher.

Copyright © 2025 by
National Learning Corporation

212 Michael Drive, Syosset, NY 11791
(516) 921-8888 • www.passbooks.com
E-mail: info@passbooks.com

PASSBOOK® SERIES

THE *PASSBOOK® SERIES* has been created to prepare applicants and candidates for the ultimate academic battlefield – the examination room.

At some time in our lives, each and every one of us may be required to take an examination – for validation, matriculation, admission, qualification, registration, certification, or licensure.

Based on the assumption that every applicant or candidate has met the basic formal educational standards, has taken the required number of courses, and read the necessary texts, the *PASSBOOK® SERIES* furnishes the one special preparation which may assure passing with confidence, instead of failing with insecurity. Examination questions – together with answers – are furnished as the basic vehicle for study so that the mysteries of the examination and its compounding difficulties may be eliminated or diminished by a sure method.

This book is meant to help you pass your examination provided that you qualify and are serious in your objective.

The entire field is reviewed through the huge store of content information which is succinctly presented through a provocative and challenging approach – the question-and-answer method.

A climate of success is established by furnishing the correct answers at the end of each test.

You soon learn to recognize types of questions, forms of questions, and patterns of questioning. You may even begin to anticipate expected outcomes.

You perceive that many questions are repeated or adapted so that you can gain acute insights, which may enable you to score many sure points.

You learn how to confront new questions, or types of questions, and to attack them confidently and work out the correct answers.

You note objectives and emphases, and recognize pitfalls and dangers, so that you may make positive educational adjustments.

Moreover, you are kept fully informed in relation to new concepts, methods, practices, and directions in the field.

You discover that you are actually taking the examination all the time: you are preparing for the examination by "taking" an examination, not by reading extraneous and/or supererogatory textbooks.

In short, this PASSBOOK®, used directedly, should be an important factor in helping you to pass your test.

INFECTION CONTROL NURSE

DUTIES
As an Infection Control Nurse, you would have responsibility of an infection control and prevention program, ensuring its adherence to established infection control standards and policies, and developing education programs for patients and staff. You would serve in a liaison capacity between all departments and Infection Control Committees or hospital departments responsible for infection control and prevention services.

SCOPE OF THE EXAMINATION
The written test will cover knowledge, skills and/or abilities in such areas as:

1. General principles of biology, epidemiology, microbiology and sanitation;
2. Infection control principles and practices;
3. Management of an infection control program; and
4. Methods in research, data analysis and basic statistics.

HOW TO TAKE A TEST

I. YOU MUST PASS AN EXAMINATION

A. WHAT EVERY CANDIDATE SHOULD KNOW

Examination applicants often ask us for help in preparing for the written test. What can I study in advance? What kinds of questions will be asked? How will the test be given? How will the papers be graded?

As an applicant for a civil service examination, you may be wondering about some of these things. Our purpose here is to suggest effective methods of advance study and to describe civil service examinations.

Your chances for success on this examination can be increased if you know how to prepare. Those "pre-examination jitters" can be reduced if you know what to expect. You can even experience an adventure in good citizenship if you know why civil service exams are given.

B. WHY ARE CIVIL SERVICE EXAMINATIONS GIVEN?

Civil service examinations are important to you in two ways. As a citizen, you want public jobs filled by employees who know how to do their work. As a job seeker, you want a fair chance to compete for that job on an equal footing with other candidates. The best-known means of accomplishing this two-fold goal is the competitive examination.

Exams are widely publicized throughout the nation. They may be administered for jobs in federal, state, city, municipal, town or village governments or agencies.

Any citizen may apply, with some limitations, such as the age or residence of applicants. Your experience and education may be reviewed to see whether you meet the requirements for the particular examination. When these requirements exist, they are reasonable and applied consistently to all applicants. Thus, a competitive examination may cause you some uneasiness now, but it is your privilege and safeguard.

C. HOW ARE CIVIL SERVICE EXAMS DEVELOPED?

Examinations are carefully written by trained technicians who are specialists in the field known as "psychological measurement," in consultation with recognized authorities in the field of work that the test will cover. These experts recommend the subject matter areas or skills to be tested; only those knowledges or skills important to your success on the job are included. The most reliable books and source materials available are used as references. Together, the experts and technicians judge the difficulty level of the questions.

Test technicians know how to phrase questions so that the problem is clearly stated. Their ethics do not permit "trick" or "catch" questions. Questions may have been tried out on sample groups, or subjected to statistical analysis, to determine their usefulness.

Written tests are often used in combination with performance tests, ratings of training and experience, and oral interviews. All of these measures combine to form the best-known means of finding the right person for the right job.

II. HOW TO PASS THE WRITTEN TEST

A. NATURE OF THE EXAMINATION

To prepare intelligently for civil service examinations, you should know how they differ from school examinations you have taken. In school you were assigned certain definite pages to read or subjects to cover. The examination questions were quite detailed and usually emphasized memory. Civil service exams, on the other hand, try to discover your present ability to perform the duties of a position, plus your potentiality to learn these duties. In other words, a civil service exam attempts to predict how successful you will be. Questions cover such a broad area that they cannot be as minute and detailed as school exam questions.

In the public service similar kinds of work, or positions, are grouped together in one "class." This process is known as *position-classification*. All the positions in a class are paid according to the salary range for that class. One class title covers all of these positions, and they are all tested by the same examination.

B. FOUR BASIC STEPS

1) Study the announcement

How, then, can you know what subjects to study? Our best answer is: "Learn as much as possible about the class of positions for which you've applied." The exam will test the knowledge, skills and abilities needed to do the work.

Your most valuable source of information about the position you want is the official exam announcement. This announcement lists the training and experience qualifications. Check these standards and apply only if you come reasonably close to meeting them.

The brief description of the position in the examination announcement offers some clues to the subjects which will be tested. Think about the job itself. Review the duties in your mind. Can you perform them, or are there some in which you are rusty? Fill in the blank spots in your preparation.

Many jurisdictions preview the written test in the exam announcement by including a section called "Knowledge and Abilities Required," "Scope of the Examination," or some similar heading. Here you will find out specifically what fields will be tested.

2) Review your own background

Once you learn in general what the position is all about, and what you need to know to do the work, ask yourself which subjects you already know fairly well and which need improvement. You may wonder whether to concentrate on improving your strong areas or on building some background in your fields of weakness. When the announcement has specified "some knowledge" or "considerable knowledge," or has used adjectives like "beginning principles of…" or "advanced … methods," you can get a clue as to the number and difficulty of questions to be asked in any given field. More questions, and hence broader coverage, would be included for those subjects which are more important in the work. Now weigh your strengths and weaknesses against the job requirements and prepare accordingly.

3) Determine the level of the position

Another way to tell how intensively you should prepare is to understand the level of the job for which you are applying. Is it the entering level? In other words, is this the position in which beginners in a field of work are hired? Or is it an intermediate or advanced level? Sometimes this is indicated by such words as "Junior" or "Senior" in the class title. Other jurisdictions use Roman numerals to designate the level – Clerk I, Clerk II, for example. The word "Supervisor" sometimes appears in the title. If the level is not indicated by the title, check the description of duties. Will you be working under very close supervision, or will you have responsibility for independent decisions in this work?

4) Choose appropriate study materials

Now that you know the subjects to be examined and the relative amount of each subject to be covered, you can choose suitable study materials. For beginning level jobs, or even advanced ones, if you have a pronounced weakness in some aspect of your training, read a modern, standard textbook in that field. Be sure it is up to date and has general coverage. Such books are normally available at your library, and the librarian will be glad to help you locate one. For entry-level positions, questions of appropriate difficulty are chosen – neither highly advanced questions, nor those too simple. Such questions require careful thought but not advanced training.

If the position for which you are applying is technical or advanced, you will read more advanced, specialized material. If you are already familiar with the basic principles of your field, elementary textbooks would waste your time. Concentrate on advanced textbooks and technical periodicals. Think through the concepts and review difficult problems in your field.

These are all general sources. You can get more ideas on your own initiative, following these leads. For example, training manuals and publications of the government agency which employs workers in your field can be useful, particularly for technical and professional positions. A letter or visit to the government department involved may result in more specific study suggestions, and certainly will provide you with a more definite idea of the exact nature of the position you are seeking.

III. KINDS OF TESTS

Tests are used for purposes other than measuring knowledge and ability to perform specified duties. For some positions, it is equally important to test ability to make adjustments to new situations or to profit from training. In others, basic mental abilities not dependent on information are essential. Questions which test these things may not appear as pertinent to the duties of the position as those which test for knowledge and information. Yet they are often highly important parts of a fair examination. For very general questions, it is almost impossible to help you direct your study efforts. What we can do is to point out some of the more common of these general abilities needed in public service positions and describe some typical questions.

1) General information

Broad, general information has been found useful for predicting job success in some kinds of work. This is tested in a variety of ways, from vocabulary lists to questions about current events. Basic background in some field of work, such as sociology or economics, may be sampled in a group of questions. Often these are principles which have become familiar to most persons through exposure rather than through formal training. It is difficult to advise you how to study for these questions; being alert to the world around you is our best suggestion.

2) Verbal ability

An example of an ability needed in many positions is verbal or language ability. Verbal ability is, in brief, the ability to use and understand words. Vocabulary and grammar tests are typical measures of this ability. Reading comprehension or paragraph interpretation questions are common in many kinds of civil service tests. You are given a paragraph of written material and asked to find its central meaning.

3) Numerical ability

Number skills can be tested by the familiar arithmetic problem, by checking paired lists of numbers to see which are alike and which are different, or by interpreting charts and graphs. In the latter test, a graph may be printed in the test booklet which you are asked to use as the basis for answering questions.

4) Observation

A popular test for law-enforcement positions is the observation test. A picture is shown to you for several minutes, then taken away. Questions about the picture test your ability to observe both details and larger elements.

5) Following directions

In many positions in the public service, the employee must be able to carry out written instructions dependably and accurately. You may be given a chart with several columns, each column listing a variety of information. The questions require you to carry out directions involving the information given in the chart.

6) Skills and aptitudes

Performance tests effectively measure some manual skills and aptitudes. When the skill is one in which you are trained, such as typing or shorthand, you can practice. These tests are often very much like those given in business school or high school courses. For many of the other skills and aptitudes, however, no short-time preparation can be made. Skills and abilities natural to you or that you have developed throughout your lifetime are being tested.

Many of the general questions just described provide all the data needed to answer the questions and ask you to use your reasoning ability to find the answers. Your best preparation for these tests, as well as for tests of facts and ideas, is to be at your physical and mental best. You, no doubt, have your own methods of getting into an exam-taking mood and keeping "in shape." The next section lists some ideas on this subject.

IV. KINDS OF QUESTIONS

Only rarely is the "essay" question, which you answer in narrative form, used in civil service tests. Civil service tests are usually of the short-answer type. Full instructions for answering these questions will be given to you at the examination. But in case this is your first experience with short-answer questions and separate answer sheets, here is what you need to know:

1) Multiple-choice Questions

Most popular of the short-answer questions is the "multiple choice" or "best answer" question. It can be used, for example, to test for factual knowledge, ability to solve problems or judgment in meeting situations found at work.

A multiple-choice question is normally one of three types—
- It can begin with an incomplete statement followed by several possible endings. You are to find the one ending which *best* completes the statement, although some of the others may not be entirely wrong.
- It can also be a complete statement in the form of a question which is answered by choosing one of the statements listed.

- It can be in the form of a problem – again you select the best answer.

Here is an example of a multiple-choice question with a discussion which should give you some clues as to the method for choosing the right answer:

When an employee has a complaint about his assignment, the action which will *best* help him overcome his difficulty is to
  A. discuss his difficulty with his coworkers
  B. take the problem to the head of the organization
  C. take the problem to the person who gave him the assignment
  D. say nothing to anyone about his complaint

In answering this question, you should study each of the choices to find which is best. Consider choice "A" – Certainly an employee may discuss his complaint with fellow employees, but no change or improvement can result, and the complaint remains unresolved. Choice "B" is a poor choice since the head of the organization probably does not know what assignment you have been given, and taking your problem to him is known as "going over the head" of the supervisor. The supervisor, or person who made the assignment, is the person who can clarify it or correct any injustice. Choice "C" is, therefore, correct. To say nothing, as in choice "D," is unwise. Supervisors have and interest in knowing the problems employees are facing, and the employee is seeking a solution to his problem.

2) True/False Questions

The "true/false" or "right/wrong" form of question is sometimes used. Here a complete statement is given. Your job is to decide whether the statement is right or wrong.

SAMPLE: A roaming cell-phone call to a nearby city costs less than a non-roaming call to a distant city.

This statement is wrong, or false, since roaming calls are more expensive.

This is not a complete list of all possible question forms, although most of the others are variations of these common types. You will always get complete directions for answering questions. Be sure you understand *how* to mark your answers – ask questions until you do.

V. RECORDING YOUR ANSWERS

Computer terminals are used more and more today for many different kinds of exams.

For an examination with very few applicants, you may be told to record your answers in the test booklet itself. Separate answer sheets are much more common. If this separate answer sheet is to be scored by machine – and this is often the case – it is highly important that you mark your answers correctly in order to get credit.

An electronic scoring machine is often used in civil service offices because of the speed with which papers can be scored. Machine-scored answer sheets must be marked with a pencil, which will be given to you. This pencil has a high graphite content which responds to the electronic scoring machine. As a matter of fact, stray dots may register as answers, so do not let your pencil rest on the answer sheet while you are pondering the correct answer. Also, if your pencil lead breaks or is otherwise defective, ask for another.

Since the answer sheet will be dropped in a slot in the scoring machine, be careful not to bend the corners or get the paper crumpled.

The answer sheet normally has five vertical columns of numbers, with 30 numbers to a column. These numbers correspond to the question numbers in your test booklet. After each number, going across the page are four or five pairs of dotted lines. These short dotted lines have small letters or numbers above them. The first two pairs may also have a "T" or "F" above the letters. This indicates that the first two pairs only are to be used if the questions are of the true-false type. If the questions are multiple choice, disregard the "T" and "F" and pay attention only to the small letters or numbers.

Answer your questions in the manner of the sample that follows:

32. The largest city in the United States is
    A. Washington, D.C.
    B. New York City
    C. Chicago
    D. Detroit
    E. San Francisco

1) Choose the answer you think is best. (New York City is the largest, so "B" is correct.)
2) Find the row of dotted lines numbered the same as the question you are answering. (Find row number 32)
3) Find the pair of dotted lines corresponding to the answer. (Find the pair of lines under the mark "B.")
4) Make a solid black mark between the dotted lines.

VI. BEFORE THE TEST

Common sense will help you find procedures to follow to get ready for an examination. Too many of us, however, overlook these sensible measures. Indeed, nervousness and fatigue have been found to be the most serious reasons why applicants fail to do their best on civil service tests. Here is a list of reminders:

- Begin your preparation early – Don't wait until the last minute to go scurrying around for books and materials or to find out what the position is all about.
- Prepare continuously – An hour a night for a week is better than an all-night cram session. This has been definitely established. What is more, a night a week for a month will return better dividends than crowding your study into a shorter period of time.
- Locate the place of the exam – You have been sent a notice telling you when and where to report for the examination. If the location is in a different town or otherwise unfamiliar to you, it would be well to inquire the best route and learn something about the building.
- Relax the night before the test – Allow your mind to rest. Do not study at all that night. Plan some mild recreation or diversion; then go to bed early and get a good night's sleep.
- Get up early enough to make a leisurely trip to the place for the test – This way unforeseen events, traffic snarls, unfamiliar buildings, etc. will not upset you.
- Dress comfortably – A written test is not a fashion show. You will be known by number and not by name, so wear something comfortable.

- Leave excess paraphernalia at home – Shopping bags and odd bundles will get in your way. You need bring only the items mentioned in the official notice you received; usually everything you need is provided. Do not bring reference books to the exam. They will only confuse those last minutes and be taken away from you when in the test room.
- Arrive somewhat ahead of time – If because of transportation schedules you must get there very early, bring a newspaper or magazine to take your mind off yourself while waiting.
- Locate the examination room – When you have found the proper room, you will be directed to the seat or part of the room where you will sit. Sometimes you are given a sheet of instructions to read while you are waiting. Do not fill out any forms until you are told to do so; just read them and be prepared.
- Relax and prepare to listen to the instructions
- If you have any physical problem that may keep you from doing your best, be sure to tell the test administrator. If you are sick or in poor health, you really cannot do your best on the exam. You can come back and take the test some other time.

VII. AT THE TEST

The day of the test is here and you have the test booklet in your hand. The temptation to get going is very strong. Caution! There is more to success than knowing the right answers. You must know how to identify your papers and understand variations in the type of short-answer question used in this particular examination. Follow these suggestions for maximum results from your efforts:

1) Cooperate with the monitor

The test administrator has a duty to create a situation in which you can be as much at ease as possible. He will give instructions, tell you when to begin, check to see that you are marking your answer sheet correctly, and so on. He is not there to guard you, although he will see that your competitors do not take unfair advantage. He wants to help you do your best.

2) Listen to all instructions

Don't jump the gun! Wait until you understand all directions. In most civil service tests you get more time than you need to answer the questions. So don't be in a hurry. Read each word of instructions until you clearly understand the meaning. Study the examples, listen to all announcements and follow directions. Ask questions if you do not understand what to do.

3) Identify your papers

Civil service exams are usually identified by number only. You will be assigned a number; you must not put your name on your test papers. Be sure to copy your number correctly. Since more than one exam may be given, copy your exact examination title.

4) Plan your time

Unless you are told that a test is a "speed" or "rate of work" test, speed itself is usually not important. Time enough to answer all the questions will be provided, but this does not mean that you have all day. An overall time limit has been set. Divide the total time (in minutes) by the number of questions to determine the approximate time you have for each question.

5) Do not linger over difficult questions

If you come across a difficult question, mark it with a paper clip (useful to have along) and come back to it when you have been through the booklet. One caution if you do this – be sure to skip a number on your answer sheet as well. Check often to be sure that you have not lost your place and that you are marking in the row numbered the same as the question you are answering.

6) Read the questions

Be sure you know what the question asks! Many capable people are unsuccessful because they failed to *read* the questions correctly.

7) Answer all questions

Unless you have been instructed that a penalty will be deducted for incorrect answers, it is better to guess than to omit a question.

8) Speed tests

It is often better NOT to guess on speed tests. It has been found that on timed tests people are tempted to spend the last few seconds before time is called in marking answers at random – without even reading them – in the hope of picking up a few extra points. To discourage this practice, the instructions may warn you that your score will be "corrected" for guessing. That is, a penalty will be applied. The incorrect answers will be deducted from the correct ones, or some other penalty formula will be used.

9) Review your answers

If you finish before time is called, go back to the questions you guessed or omitted to give them further thought. Review other answers if you have time.

10) Return your test materials

If you are ready to leave before others have finished or time is called, take ALL your materials to the monitor and leave quietly. Never take any test material with you. The monitor can discover whose papers are not complete, and taking a test booklet may be grounds for disqualification.

VIII. EXAMINATION TECHNIQUES

1) Read the general instructions carefully. These are usually printed on the first page of the exam booklet. As a rule, these instructions refer to the timing of the examination; the fact that you should not start work until the signal and must stop work at a signal, etc. If there are any *special* instructions, such as a choice of questions to be answered, make sure that you note this instruction carefully.

2) When you are ready to start work on the examination, that is as soon as the signal has been given, read the instructions to each question booklet, underline any key words or phrases, such as *least, best, outline, describe* and the like. In this way you will tend to answer as requested rather than discover on reviewing your paper that you *listed without describing*, that you selected the *worst* choice rather than the *best* choice, etc.

3) If the examination is of the objective or multiple-choice type – that is, each question will also give a series of possible answers: A, B, C or D, and you are called upon to select the best answer and write the letter next to that answer on your answer paper – it is advisable to start answering each question in turn. There may be anywhere from 50 to 100 such questions in the three or four hours allotted and you can see how much time would be taken if you read through all the questions before beginning to answer any. Furthermore, if you come across a question or group of questions which you know would be difficult to answer, it would undoubtedly affect your handling of all the other questions.

4) If the examination is of the essay type and contains but a few questions, it is a moot point as to whether you should read all the questions before starting to answer any one. Of course, if you are given a choice – say five out of seven and the like – then it is essential to read all the questions so you can eliminate the two that are most difficult. If, however, you are asked to answer all the questions, there may be danger in trying to answer the easiest one first because you may find that you will spend too much time on it. The best technique is to answer the first question, then proceed to the second, etc.

5) Time your answers. Before the exam begins, write down the time it started, then add the time allowed for the examination and write down the time it must be completed, then divide the time available somewhat as follows:
   - If 3-1/2 hours are allowed, that would be 210 minutes. If you have 80 objective-type questions, that would be an average of 2-1/2 minutes per question. Allow yourself no more than 2 minutes per question, or a total of 160 minutes, which will permit about 50 minutes to review.
   - If for the time allotment of 210 minutes there are 7 essay questions to answer, that would average about 30 minutes a question. Give yourself only 25 minutes per question so that you have about 35 minutes to review.

6) The most important instruction is to *read each question* and make sure you know what is wanted. The second most important instruction is to *time yourself properly* so that you answer every question. The third most important instruction is to *answer every question*. Guess if you have to but include something for each question. Remember that you will receive no credit for a blank and will probably receive some credit if you write something in answer to an essay question. If you guess a letter – say "B" for a multiple-choice question – you may have guessed right. If you leave a blank as an answer to a multiple-choice question, the examiners may respect your feelings but it will not add a point to your score. Some exams may penalize you for wrong answers, so in such cases *only*, you may not want to guess unless you have some basis for your answer.

7) Suggestions
   a. Objective-type questions
      1. Examine the question booklet for proper sequence of pages and questions
      2. Read all instructions carefully
      3. Skip any question which seems too difficult; return to it after all other questions have been answered
      4. Apportion your time properly; do not spend too much time on any single question or group of questions

5. Note and underline key words – *all, most, fewest, least, best, worst, same, opposite,* etc.
6. Pay particular attention to negatives
7. Note unusual option, e.g., unduly long, short, complex, different or similar in content to the body of the question
8. Observe the use of "hedging" words – *probably, may, most likely,* etc.
9. Make sure that your answer is put next to the same number as the question
10. Do not second-guess unless you have good reason to believe the second answer is definitely more correct
11. Cross out original answer if you decide another answer is more accurate; do not erase until you are ready to hand your paper in
12. Answer all questions; guess unless instructed otherwise
13. Leave time for review

b. Essay questions
1. Read each question carefully
2. Determine exactly what is wanted. Underline key words or phrases.
3. Decide on outline or paragraph answer
4. Include many different points and elements unless asked to develop any one or two points or elements
5. Show impartiality by giving pros and cons unless directed to select one side only
6. Make and write down any assumptions you find necessary to answer the questions
7. Watch your English, grammar, punctuation and choice of words
8. Time your answers; don't crowd material

8) Answering the essay question

Most essay questions can be answered by framing the specific response around several key words or ideas. Here are a few such key words or ideas:

M's: manpower, materials, methods, money, management
P's: purpose, program, policy, plan, procedure, practice, problems, pitfalls, personnel, public relations

a. Six basic steps in handling problems:
1. Preliminary plan and background development
2. Collect information, data and facts
3. Analyze and interpret information, data and facts
4. Analyze and develop solutions as well as make recommendations
5. Prepare report and sell recommendations
6. Install recommendations and follow up effectiveness

b. Pitfalls to avoid
1. *Taking things for granted* – A statement of the situation does not necessarily imply that each of the elements is necessarily true; for example, a complaint may be invalid and biased so that all that can be taken for granted is that a complaint has been registered

2. *Considering only one side of a situation* – Wherever possible, indicate several alternatives and then point out the reasons you selected the best one
3. *Failing to indicate follow up* – Whenever your answer indicates action on your part, make certain that you will take proper follow-up action to see how successful your recommendations, procedures or actions turn out to be
4. *Taking too long in answering any single question* – Remember to time your answers properly

IX. AFTER THE TEST

Scoring procedures differ in detail among civil service jurisdictions although the general principles are the same. Whether the papers are hand-scored or graded by machine we have described, they are nearly always graded by number. That is, the person who marks the paper knows only the number – never the name – of the applicant. Not until all the papers have been graded will they be matched with names. If other tests, such as training and experience or oral interview ratings have been given, scores will be combined. Different parts of the examination usually have different weights. For example, the written test might count 60 percent of the final grade, and a rating of training and experience 40 percent. In many jurisdictions, veterans will have a certain number of points added to their grades.

After the final grade has been determined, the names are placed in grade order and an eligible list is established. There are various methods for resolving ties between those who get the same final grade – probably the most common is to place first the name of the person whose application was received first. Job offers are made from the eligible list in the order the names appear on it. You will be notified of your grade and your rank as soon as all these computations have been made. This will be done as rapidly as possible.

People who are found to meet the requirements in the announcement are called "eligibles." Their names are put on a list of eligible candidates. An eligible's chances of getting a job depend on how high he stands on this list and how fast agencies are filling jobs from the list.

When a job is to be filled from a list of eligibles, the agency asks for the names of people on the list of eligibles for that job. When the civil service commission receives this request, it sends to the agency the names of the three people highest on this list. Or, if the job to be filled has specialized requirements, the office sends the agency the names of the top three persons who meet these requirements from the general list.

The appointing officer makes a choice from among the three people whose names were sent to him. If the selected person accepts the appointment, the names of the others are put back on the list to be considered for future openings.

That is the rule in hiring from all kinds of eligible lists, whether they are for typist, carpenter, chemist, or something else. For every vacancy, the appointing officer has his choice of any one of the top three eligibles on the list. This explains why the person whose name is on top of the list sometimes does not get an appointment when some of the persons lower on the list do. If the appointing officer chooses the second or third eligible, the No. 1 eligible does not get a job at once, but stays on the list until he is appointed or the list is terminated.

X. HOW TO PASS THE INTERVIEW TEST

The examination for which you applied requires an oral interview test. You have already taken the written test and you are now being called for the interview test – the final part of the formal examination.

You may think that it is not possible to prepare for an interview test and that there are no procedures to follow during an interview. Our purpose is to point out some things you can do in advance that will help you and some good rules to follow and pitfalls to avoid while you are being interviewed.

What is an interview supposed to test?

The written examination is designed to test the technical knowledge and competence of the candidate; the oral is designed to evaluate intangible qualities, not readily measured otherwise, and to establish a list showing the relative fitness of each candidate – as measured against his competitors – for the position sought. Scoring is not on the basis of "right" and "wrong," but on a sliding scale of values ranging from "not passable" to "outstanding." As a matter of fact, it is possible to achieve a relatively low score without a single "incorrect" answer because of evident weakness in the qualities being measured.

Occasionally, an examination may consist entirely of an oral test – either an individual or a group oral. In such cases, information is sought concerning the technical knowledges and abilities of the candidate, since there has been no written examination for this purpose. More commonly, however, an oral test is used to supplement a written examination.

Who conducts interviews?

The composition of oral boards varies among different jurisdictions. In nearly all, a representative of the personnel department serves as chairman. One of the members of the board may be a representative of the department in which the candidate would work. In some cases, "outside experts" are used, and, frequently, a businessman or some other representative of the general public is asked to serve. Labor and management or other special groups may be represented. The aim is to secure the services of experts in the appropriate field.

However the board is composed, it is a good idea (and not at all improper or unethical) to ascertain in advance of the interview who the members are and what groups they represent. When you are introduced to them, you will have some idea of their backgrounds and interests, and at least you will not stutter and stammer over their names.

What should be done before the interview?

While knowledge about the board members is useful and takes some of the surprise element out of the interview, there is other preparation which is more substantive. It *is* possible to prepare for an oral interview – in several ways:

1) Keep a copy of your application and review it carefully before the interview

This may be the only document before the oral board, and the starting point of the interview. Know what education and experience you have listed there, and the sequence and dates of all of it. Sometimes the board will ask you to review the highlights of your experience for them; you should not have to hem and haw doing it.

2) Study the class specification and the examination announcement

Usually, the oral board has one or both of these to guide them. The qualities, characteristics or knowledges required by the position sought are stated in these documents. They offer valuable clues as to the nature of the oral interview. For example, if the job involves supervisory responsibilities, the announcement will usually indicate that knowledge of modern supervisory methods and the qualifications of the candidate as a supervisor will be tested. If so, you can expect such questions, frequently in the form of a hypothetical situation which you are expected to solve. NEVER go into an oral without knowledge of the duties and responsibilities of the job you seek.

3) Think through each qualification required

Try to visualize the kind of questions you would ask if you were a board member. How well could you answer them? Try especially to appraise your own knowledge and background in each area, *measured against the job sought*, and identify any areas in which you are weak. Be critical and realistic – do not flatter yourself.

4) Do some general reading in areas in which you feel you may be weak

For example, if the job involves supervision and your past experience has NOT, some general reading in supervisory methods and practices, particularly in the field of human relations, might be useful. Do NOT study agency procedures or detailed manuals. The oral board will be testing your understanding and capacity, not your memory.

5) Get a good night's sleep and watch your general health and mental attitude

You will want a clear head at the interview. Take care of a cold or any other minor ailment, and of course, no hangovers.

What should be done on the day of the interview?

Now comes the day of the interview itself. Give yourself plenty of time to get there. Plan to arrive somewhat ahead of the scheduled time, particularly if your appointment is in the fore part of the day. If a previous candidate fails to appear, the board might be ready for you a bit early. By early afternoon an oral board is almost invariably behind schedule if there are many candidates, and you may have to wait. Take along a book or magazine to read, or your application to review, but leave any extraneous material in the waiting room when you go in for your interview. In any event, relax and compose yourself.

The matter of dress is important. The board is forming impressions about you – from your experience, your manners, your attitude, and your appearance. Give your personal appearance careful attention. Dress your best, but not your flashiest. Choose conservative, appropriate clothing, and be sure it is immaculate. This is a business interview, and your appearance should indicate that you regard it as such. Besides, being well groomed and properly dressed will help boost your confidence.

Sooner or later, someone will call your name and escort you into the interview room. *This is it.* From here on you are on your own. It is too late for any more preparation. But remember, you asked for this opportunity to prove your fitness, and you are here because your request was granted.

What happens when you go in?

The usual sequence of events will be as follows: The clerk (who is often the board stenographer) will introduce you to the chairman of the oral board, who will introduce you to the other members of the board. Acknowledge the introductions before you sit down. Do not be surprised if you find a microphone facing you or a stenotypist sitting by. Oral interviews are usually recorded in the event of an appeal or other review.

Usually the chairman of the board will open the interview by reviewing the highlights of your education and work experience from your application – primarily for the benefit of the other members of the board, as well as to get the material into the record. Do not interrupt or comment unless there is an error or significant misinterpretation; if that is the case, do not hesitate. But do not quibble about insignificant matters. Also, he will usually ask you some question about your education, experience or your present job – partly to get you to start talking and to establish the interviewing "rapport." He may start the actual questioning, or turn it over to one of the other members. Frequently, each member undertakes the questioning on a particular area, one in which he is perhaps most competent, so you can expect each member to participate in the examination. Because time is limited, you may also expect some rather abrupt switches in the direction the questioning takes, so do not be upset by it. Normally, a board member will not pursue a single line of questioning unless he discovers a particular strength or weakness.

After each member has participated, the chairman will usually ask whether any member has any further questions, then will ask you if you have anything you wish to add. Unless you are expecting this question, it may floor you. Worse, it may start you off on an extended, extemporaneous speech. The board is not usually seeking more information. The question is principally to offer you a last opportunity to present further qualifications or to indicate that you have nothing to add. So, if you feel that a significant qualification or characteristic has been overlooked, it is proper to point it out in a sentence or so. Do not compliment the board on the thoroughness of their examination – they have been sketchy, and you know it. If you wish, merely say, "No thank you, I have nothing further to add." This is a point where you can "talk yourself out" of a good impression or fail to present an important bit of information. Remember, *you close the interview yourself*.

The chairman will then say, "That is all, Mr. _____, thank you." Do not be startled; the interview is over, and quicker than you think. Thank him, gather your belongings and take your leave. Save your sigh of relief for the other side of the door.

How to put your best foot forward

Throughout this entire process, you may feel that the board individually and collectively is trying to pierce your defenses, seek out your hidden weaknesses and embarrass and confuse you. Actually, this is not true. They are obliged to make an appraisal of your qualifications for the job you are seeking, and they want to see you in your best light. Remember, they must interview all candidates and a non-cooperative candidate may become a failure in spite of their best efforts to bring out his qualifications. Here are 15 suggestions that will help you:

1) **Be natural – Keep your attitude confident, not cocky**

If you are not confident that you can do the job, do not expect the board to be. Do not apologize for your weaknesses, try to bring out your strong points. The board is interested in a positive, not negative, presentation. Cockiness will antagonize any board member and make him wonder if you are covering up a weakness by a false show of strength.

2) **Get comfortable, but don't lounge or sprawl**

Sit erectly but not stiffly. A careless posture may lead the board to conclude that you are careless in other things, or at least that you are not impressed by the importance of the occasion. Either conclusion is natural, even if incorrect. Do not fuss with your clothing, a pencil or an ashtray. Your hands may occasionally be useful to emphasize a point; do not let them become a point of distraction.

3) **Do not wisecrack or make small talk**

This is a serious situation, and your attitude should show that you consider it as such. Further, the time of the board is limited – they do not want to waste it, and neither should you.

4) Do not exaggerate your experience or abilities

In the first place, from information in the application or other interviews and sources, the board may know more about you than you think. Secondly, you probably will not get away with it. An experienced board is rather adept at spotting such a situation, so do not take the chance.

5) If you know a board member, do not make a point of it, yet do not hide it

Certainly you are not fooling him, and probably not the other members of the board. Do not try to take advantage of your acquaintanceship – it will probably do you little good.

6) Do not dominate the interview

Let the board do that. They will give you the clues – do not assume that you have to do all the talking. Realize that the board has a number of questions to ask you, and do not try to take up all the interview time by showing off your extensive knowledge of the answer to the first one.

7) Be attentive

You only have 20 minutes or so, and you should keep your attention at its sharpest throughout. When a member is addressing a problem or question to you, give him your undivided attention. Address your reply principally to him, but do not exclude the other board members.

8) Do not interrupt

A board member may be stating a problem for you to analyze. He will ask you a question when the time comes. Let him state the problem, and wait for the question.

9) Make sure you understand the question

Do not try to answer until you are sure what the question is. If it is not clear, restate it in your own words or ask the board member to clarify it for you. However, do not haggle about minor elements.

10) Reply promptly but not hastily

A common entry on oral board rating sheets is "candidate responded readily," or "candidate hesitated in replies." Respond as promptly and quickly as you can, but do not jump to a hasty, ill-considered answer.

11) Do not be peremptory in your answers

A brief answer is proper – but do not fire your answer back. That is a losing game from your point of view. The board member can probably ask questions much faster than you can answer them.

12) Do not try to create the answer you think the board member wants

He is interested in what kind of mind you have and how it works – not in playing games. Furthermore, he can usually spot this practice and will actually grade you down on it.

13) Do not switch sides in your reply merely to agree with a board member

Frequently, a member will take a contrary position merely to draw you out and to see if you are willing and able to defend your point of view. Do not start a debate, yet do not surrender a good position. If a position is worth taking, it is worth defending.

14) Do not be afraid to admit an error in judgment if you are shown to be wrong

The board knows that you are forced to reply without any opportunity for careful consideration. Your answer may be demonstrably wrong. If so, admit it and get on with the interview.

15) Do not dwell at length on your present job

The opening question may relate to your present assignment. Answer the question but do not go into an extended discussion. You are being examined for a *new* job, not your present one. As a matter of fact, try to phrase ALL your answers in terms of the job for which you are being examined.

Basis of Rating

Probably you will forget most of these "do's" and "don'ts" when you walk into the oral interview room. Even remembering them all will not ensure you a passing grade. Perhaps you did not have the qualifications in the first place. But remembering them will help you to put your best foot forward, without treading on the toes of the board members.

Rumor and popular opinion to the contrary notwithstanding, an oral board wants you to make the best appearance possible. They know you are under pressure – but they also want to see how you respond to it as a guide to what your reaction would be under the pressures of the job you seek. They will be influenced by the degree of poise you display, the personal traits you show and the manner in which you respond.

ABOUT THIS BOOK

This book contains tests divided into Examination Sections. Go through each test, answering every question in the margin. We have also attached a sample answer sheet at the back of the book that can be removed and used. At the end of each test look at the answer key and check your answers. On the ones you got wrong, look at the right answer choice and learn. Do not fill in the answers first. Do not memorize the questions and answers, but understand the answer and principles involved. On your test, the questions will likely be different from the samples. Questions are changed and new ones added. If you understand these past questions you should have success with any changes that arise. Tests may consist of several types of questions. We have additional books on each subject should more study be advisable or necessary for you. Finally, the more you study, the better prepared you will be. This book is intended to be the last thing you study before you walk into the examination room. Prior study of relevant texts is also recommended. NLC publishes some of these in our Fundamental Series. Knowledge and good sense are important factors in passing your exam. Good luck also helps. So now study this Passbook, absorb the material contained within and take that knowledge into the examination. Then do your best to pass that exam.

EXAMINATION SECTION

EXAMINATION SECTION
TEST 1

DIRECTIONS: Each question or incomplete statement is followed by several suggested answers or completions. Select the one that BEST answers the question or completes the statement. *PRINT THE LETTER OF THE CORRECT ANSWER IN THE SPACE AT THE RIGHT.*

1. _____ disinfection uses heat to kill all microorganisms with the exception of spores.
   A. Ultraviolet   B. Ultrasonic   C. Thermal   D. Ozone

2. What type of solution inhibits the growth of bacteria and is typically used topically only on animate objects?
   A. Antiseptic   B. Disinfectant   C. Bactericide   D. Fungicide

3. _____ are often pathogenic to humans because they grow best at body temperature.
   A. Extremophiles
   B. Thermophiles
   C. Mesophiles
   D. Psyhchrophiles

4. What technique should be used for brushing instruments?
   A. Brushing should be done under water
   B. Brushing should be done above water
   C. Brushing against the grain of the device
   D. Brushing should be performed only with wire brushes

5. The final rinse water used for cleaning should be treated through which of the following systems?
   A. Water conductivity
   B. Sanitation
   C. Deionization
   D. Sterilization

6. Which product is used to kill microorganisms?
   A. Detergents
   B. Germicidal detergents
   C. Soaps
   D. Enzyme Presoaks

7. _____ in water can be removed by water softeners.
   A. Iron and Chloride
   B. Calcium and Magnesium
   C. Iron and Pyrogens
   D. Silicates and Pyrogens

8. The ideal chloride concentration for tap water is _____ ppm or less.
   A. 50   B. 100   C. 150   D. 200

9. Water purification is normally performed through the use of which of the following?
   A. Pre-filter
   B. Post-filter
   C. Pre-filter or Post-filter
   D. Pre-filter and Post-filter

1.____
2.____
3.____
4.____
5.____
6.____
7.____
8.____
9.____

10. Turbid water has what kind of appearance?
    A. Clear   B. Particulate   C. Cloudy   D. Soapy

11. When should the process of pre-cleaning be initiated?
    A. Prior to items being sorted
    B. Immediately after instruments are inspected
    C. Upon receipt of the devices in the Central Services Area
    D. Immediately upon completion of an invasive procedure

12. The ideal silicate level in water used for cleaning is _____ ppm or less.
    A. 50   B. 100   C. 150   D. 200

13. Which process requires the use of deionized water?
    A. Rapid infusions   B. Sterile irrigation
    C. Steam sterilization   D. Heating/cooling therapy units

14. Which type of water impurity will result in bluish or rainbow-like stains?
    A. Calcium   B. Fluoride
    C. Chlorides and Solids   D. Iron and Silicates

15. Which of the following is the primary purpose for using manual cleaners?
    A. Removing soil
    B. Killing microorganisms
    C. Reducing the cost associated with cleaning
    D. Should only be used if automated cleaning equipment is malfunctioning

16. For what is multi-enzymatic cleaning products containing lipase useful for cleaning?
    A. Sugars   B. Fats   C. Starches   D. Proteins

17. What is the appropriate pH for purified water?
    A. 4.5 - 5.5   B. 5.5 - 6.5   C. 6.5 - 7.5   D. 7.5 - 8.5

18. Entoxins, pyrogens, and bacteria can be removed from water using which process?
    A. Reverse osmosis   B. Aeration
    C. Electronic purification D. Dissolved oxygen generation

19. Which of the following can be classified as regulated medical waste?
    A. Discarded sterilization wraps
    B. Blood-soaked sponges
    C. General trash from the operating room
    D. Spent copier toner cartridges

20. Which of the following are commonly used to break down fatty tissue on instruments?
    A. Amylase enzymes   B. Lipase enzymes
    C. Protease enzymes   D. Neutral pH cleaners

21. All of the following is accurate regarding the use of mechanical washers EXCEPT
    A. Trays with lids should be opened
    B. Multi-level trays should be separated
    C. Instruments should be disassembled and opened
    D. All items should be washed on the same cycle

    21.____

22. For what reason should the water be degassed each time the tank of an ultrasonic cleaner is changed?
    Excess bubbles
    A. from the filling process reduce the energy of the cavitation process
    B. decrease the temperature of the tank
    C. make it difficult to see the items being cleaned
    D. reduce the effectiveness of the detergent

    22.____

23. Specialized clothing or equipment worn by an employee for protection against biological hazards is referred to as
    A. personal protective equipment
    B. hazard equipment
    C. restricted apparel
    D. safety apparel

    23.____

24. What is the appropriate method for cleaning aluminum items?
    A. Using a stiff metal brush
    B. Using a water spray
    C. Using a circular motion
    D. Using a *to and fro* motion with the grain

    24.____

25. Which of the following is TRUE regarding softened water?
    A. Increases the likelihood of mineral scale deposits
    B. Decreases the likelihood of mineral scale deposits
    C. Is not compatible with detergents
    D. Can cause rusting in metal instruments

    25.____

KEY (CORRECT ANSWERS)

1.	C	11.	D
2.	A	12.	B
3.	C	13.	D
4.	A	14.	D
5.	C	15.	A
6.	B	16.	B
7.	C	17.	C
8.	B	18.	A
9.	A	19.	B
10.	C	20.	C

21. D
22. A
23. A
24. D
25. C

TEST 2

DIRECTIONS: Each question or incomplete statement is followed by several suggested answers or completions. Select the one that BEST answers the question or completes the statement. *PRINT THE LETTER OF THE CORRECT ANSWER IN THE SPACE AT THE RIGHT.*

1. Which of the following is FALSE regarding powered surgical instruments? 1.____
    A. Can be immersed
    B. Cannot be immersed
    C. Should be cleaned using a mechanical washer
    D. Should be cleaned at the point of use

2. What entity should provide the written cleaning instructions for surgical instruments? 2.____
    A. Manufacturer of the instrument
    B. The healthcare facility
    C. Manufacturer of the mechanical washer
    D. Manufacturer of the detergent

3. Which of the following is TRUE regarding pyrogens? 3.____
    A. They are fever producing substances.
    B. They are soil particles.
    C. They cause CD.
    D. They are microorganisms that remain after the sterilization process.

4. What is the appropriate pH level for detergents used for the majority of cleaning processes? 4.____
    A. High pH
    B. Low pH
    C. Neutral pH
    D. Varies according to water temperature and exposure time

5. When should instrument lubrication be performed? 5.____
    A. Immediately prior to use   B. Prior to cleaning
    C. After cleaning   D. After sterilization

6. What is the appropriate water temperature in order to avoid the coagulation of proteins? 6.____
    A. Below 24°C   B. Below 43°C   C. Above 43°C   D. Below 100°C

7. Which is the appropriate solution for cleaning instruments? 7.____
    A. Soap   B. Steam   C. Disinfectant   D. Detergent

8. Detergents used in mechanical cleaners should have which of the following characteristics? 8.____
    A. Low acidity   B. Low alkalinity
    C. Low foaming   D. Low temperature

9. Which of the following is classified as a high level disinfectant?
    A. Halogens and OPA
    B. Quaternary Ammonium Compounds and Phenolics
    C. Gluteraldehyde and OPA
    D. Gluteraldehyde and Phenolics

9.____

10. Which of the following is used during the thermal disinfection process?
    A. High pressure steam
    B. Heated water
    C. Heated gluteraldehyde
    D. Heated chemicals

10.____

11. Iodophors are a member of which disinfectant family?
    A. Halogens
    B. Alcohol
    C. Phenolics
    D. Quaternary Ammonium Compounds

11.____

12. Which process is used to completely destroy all forms of microorganisms?
    A. High-level disinfection
    B. Thermal disinfection
    C. Chemical disinfection
    D. Sterilization

12.____

13. For what time period must alcohol remain in wet contact with an item in order to achieve a reasonable level of disinfection?
    A. 3 minutes   B. 5 minutes   C. 10 minutes   D. 20 minutes

13.____

14. How are phenolics classified?
    A. Sterilants
    B. Intermediate to low-level disinfectants
    C. Intermediate to high-level disinfectants
    D. High-level disinfectants

14.____

15. Which chemicals are used on living tissue to slow the growth of micro-organisms?
    A. Antiseptics
    B. Disinfectants
    C. Gluteraldehydes
    D. Halogens

15.____

16. Which of the following are items that are introduced directly into the bloodstream or other normally sterile areas of the body?
    A. Immersible items
    B. Non-critical items
    C. Critical items
    D. Semi-critical items

16.____

17. What would be the BEST choice for high level disinfection of instruments?
    A. Iodophors   B. Phenolics   C. OPA   D. Chlorine

17.____

18. Thread-like tails attached to cells that permit bacteria to move through liquids are known as
    A. cytoplasm   B. tentacles   C. flagella   D. mitochondria

18.____

19. What type of stain test would be performed in order to identify bacterial traits?
    A. Ziehl-Neelsen
    B. Endospore
    C. Romanowsky
    D. Silver

    19._____

20. Microorganisms that are capable of forming a thick wall around themselves that enables them to survive in adverse conditions are referred to as
    A. microbes
    B. spores
    C. viruses
    D. fungi

    20._____

21. Cocci bacteria have what kind of shape?
    A. Cone
    B. Rod
    C. Spiral
    D. Spherical

    21._____

22. Bacillus bacteria have what kind of shape?
    A. Cone
    B. Rod
    C. Spiral
    D. Spherical

    22._____

23. Spirillum bacteria have what kind of shape?
    A. Cone
    B. Rod
    C. Spiral
    D. Spherical

    23._____

24. What is the typical method for bacterial reproduction?
    A. Baeocyte Production
    B. Binary Fission
    C. Budding
    D. Intracellular offspring production

    24._____

25. _____ bacteria are capable of growing in the absence of free oxygen.
    A. Aerobic
    B. Anaerobic
    C. Mesophilic
    D. Hydrophobic

    25._____

KEY (CORRECT ANSWERS)

1.	B	11.	A
2.	A	12.	D
3.	A	13.	B
4.	C	14.	B
5.	C	15.	A
6.	B	16.	C
7.	D	17.	B
8.	C	18.	C
9.	C	19.	A
10.	B	20.	B

21. D
22. B
23. C
24. B
25. B

TEST 3

DIRECTIONS: Each question or incomplete statement is followed by several suggested answers or completions. Select the one that BEST answers the question or completes the statement. *PRINT THE LETTER OF THE CORRECT ANSWER IN THE SPACE AT THE RIGHT.*

1. What percentage of hospital in-patients will eventually develop a nosocomial (hospital-acquired) infection?
   A. 5%   B. 10%   C. 15%   D. 25%
1.____

2. The invasion of the human body tissue by microorganisms which multiply and produce a reaction is known as
   A. anaphylaxis   B. metastasis   C. infection   D. manifestation
2.____

3. What is the minimum length of time Central Service Technicians should scrub their hands during a routine hand washing?
   A. 15 seconds   B. 30 seconds   C. 45 seconds   D. 60 seconds
3.____

4. What is the recommended temperature for the decontamination area of Central Service?
   A. 40 - 45°F   B. 50 - 55°F   C. 60 – 65°F   D. 70 - 75°F
4.____

5. _____ is defined as an inanimate object that can transmit bacteria.
   A. Thermite   B. Dendrite   C. Fomite   D. Nitrite
5.____

6. The functional center of a cell that governs activity and heredity is known as
   A. nucleolus   B. flagella   C. cytoplasm   D. nucleus
6.____

7. The Ziehl-Neelsen stain is designed to classify bacteria according to which of the following?
   A. Appearance   B. Shape   C. Size   D. Color change
7.____

8. Using gram-stain classifications, Staphylococcus, Enterococcus, and Streptococcus are all examples of gram-_____ bacteria.
   A. negative   B. positive   C. neutral   D. apparent
8.____

9. _____ is defined as the state of being soiled or infected by contact with infectious organisms or other material.
   A. Contaminated   B. Infested   C. Delineated   D. Permeated
9.____

10. What is the size of the majority of bacteria?
   A. 1 – 2 microns   B. 3 – 4 microns
   C. 5 – 6 microns   D. 6 – 7 microns
10.____

11. Sunlight is lethal to pathogens in which stage?
   A. Reproductive   B. Active
   C. Transmission   D. Vegetative
11.____

12. The process of removing ions that have an electrical charge is referred to as
    A. reionizing   B. deionizing   C. neutralizing   D. vaporizing

13. Which of the following refers to compounds that contain a positive electrical charge and exhibit germicidal properties?
    A. Anionic   B. Cationic   C. Ionizing   D. Deionizing

14. A disinfectant is a chemical that kills the majority of pathogenic organisms EXCEPT
    A. fungi   B. viruses   C. bacteria   D. spores

15. Which of the following refers to compounds that have a negative electrical charge and form a large group of synthetic detergents?
    A. Anionic   B. Cationic   C. Ionizing   D. Deionizing

16. Which disinfectant is often used for environmental sanitation on objects such as floors, walls, and furniture and is incompatible with soaps?
    A. Gluteraldehyde
    B. Alcohol
    C. Ortho-Phthaldehyde
    D. Quaternary Ammonium Compounds

17. Which disinfectant is used for semi-critical devices such as endoscopes and has sterilant capabilities?
    A. Gluteraldehyde
    B. Alcohol
    C. Ortho-Phthaldehyde
    D. Quaternary Ammonium Compounds

18. Which disinfectant has been in use for many years, is often used to disinfect equipment, and is inactivated by organic soil?
    A. Gluteraldehyde
    B. Alcohol
    C. Ortho-Phthaldehyde
    D. Quaternary Ammonium Compounds

19. Which disinfectant is effective at room temperature, provides a fast and effective method for disinfecting a wide range of items, has high-level disinfection capabilities, but is not classified as a sterilant?
    A. Gluteraldehyde
    B. Alcohol
    C. Ortho-Phthaldehyde
    D. Quaternary Ammonium Compounds

20. The process of destruction of nearly all pathogenic microorganisms on an inanimate surface is referred to as
    A. disinfection   B. sterilization
    C. washing   D. decontamination

21. Which of the following is defined as the destruction of bacteria?
    A. Germicide
    B. Fungicide
    C. Bactericide
    D. Fomicide

22. Which of the following is defined as a small, proteinaceous, infectious disease causing agent that is believed to be the smallest infectious particle?   22.____
    A. Fungi   B. Viruses   C. Bacteria   D. Prions

23. Which of the following is responsible for causing spongiform encephalopathy and Creutzfeltdt-Jakob disease?   23.____
    A. Fungi   B. Viruses   C. Bacteria   D. Prions

24. Fingernail, tissues, and money are all examples of which of the following?   24.____
    A. Fomites   B. Bacteria   C. Fungi   D. Viruses

25. During the final step in handwashing, the fingers should be rinsed with the fingertips in which direction?   25.____
    A. Up
    B. Down
    C. Parallel to the floor
    D. Intertwined

KEY (CORRECT ANSWERS)

1.	B	11.	D
2.	C	12.	B
3.	A	13.	B
4.	C	14.	D
5.	C	15.	A
6.	D	16.	D
7.	D	17.	A
8.	B	18.	B
9.	A	19.	C
10.	A	20.	A

21.	C
22.	D
23.	D
24.	A
25.	A

TEST 4

DIRECTIONS: Each question or incomplete statement is followed by several suggested answers or completions. Select the one that BEST answers the question or completes the statement. *PRINT THE LETTER OF THE CORRECT ANSWER IN THE SPACE AT THE RIGHT.*

1. The most effective waterless hand antiseptics contain what concentration of alcohol?
   A. 30 – 50%   B. 45 – 60%   C. 50 – 75%   D. 60 – 90%

2. Which of the following is defined as the removal of contamination from an item to the extent necessary for further processing?
   A. Disinfection
   B. Cleaning
   C. Sterilization
   D. Decontamination

3. How often should floors and work surfaces be cleaned?
   A. Hourly   B. Daily   C. Weekly   D. Bi-weekly

4. Which of the following statements is TRUE regarding the use of personal protective equipment in a decontamination area?
   A. The use of personal protective equipment is optional.
   B. Vinyl gloves is all that is required.
   C. Failure to wear personal protective equipment may result in disciplinary action.
   D. Gowns should be worn unless temperature is too warm.

5. Which of the following should be obtained prior to cleaning and processing a medical device?
   A. Soap and water
   B. Alcohol and acetone
   C. Hospital policy on device processing
   D. Manufacturer's guidelines on device processing

6. All of the following should be considerations when selecting a detergent EXCEPT
   A. quality of water
   B. amount of soil
   C. water temperature
   D. cost of detergent

7. The clostridium botulinum bacteria is harbored in which of the following?
   A. Food   B. Soil   C. Air   D. Water

8. A solution with a pH level of 4 is considered to be
   A. neutral   B. acidic   C. alkaline   D. contaminated

9. A solution with a pH level of 12 is considered to be
   A. neutral   B. acidic   C. alkaline   D. contaminated

10. Which of the following are major non-living reservoirs for infectious diseases?
    A. Soil and gas
    B. Oil and water
    C. Gas and oil
    D. Soil and water

    10.____

11. Why are alkaline detergents the BEST choice for mechanical washers?
    A. Increased friction during washing
    B. Decreased friction during washing
    C. Alkaline detergents should not be used by humans
    D. Acidic detergents promote corrosion within the mechanical washer

    11.____

12. _____ detergent would be the proper detergent for removing severe stains on stainless steel instruments.
    A. Organic acid
    B. Organic alkaline
    C. Proteolytic enzyme
    D. Lipolytic enzyme

    12.____

13. In order to prevent the formation of biofilm on instruments, the instruments should be rinsed with which of the following?
    A. Alcohol
    B. Saline
    C. Sterile water
    D. Distilled water

    13.____

14. For what type of instrument would an ultrasonic lumen cleaner be used to clean?
    A. Laparoscopic instruments
    B. Endoscopic instruments
    C. Feeding tubes
    D. Sternal saws

    14.____

15. Which is the proper process for mechanical washers to reduce the potential for instrument corrosion?
    A. Acid wash, alkaline rinse, regular rinse
    B. Alkaline wash, acid rinse, regular rinse
    C. Acid wash, acid rinse, regular rinse
    D. Alkaline wash, alkaline rinse, regular rinse

    15.____

16. A biological indicator should contain how many spores?
    A. 10^1
    B. 10^4
    C. 10^6
    D. 10^8

    16.____

17. Which of the following is a resistant, dormant structure that is formed inside of some bacteria and can withstand adverse conditions?
    A. Fomite
    B. Spore
    C. Endospore
    D. Exospore

    17.____

18. Which piece of equipment loosens and removes debris through the use of sound waves traveling through liquid?
    A. Autoclave
    B. Ultrasonic cleaner
    C. Mechanical washer
    D. Hydrosonic cleaner

    18.____

19. With what solution would you rinse instruments that have been processed in a liquid chemical sterilant?
    A. Alcohol
    B. Distilled water
    C. Sterile water
    D. Warm, soapy water

    19.____

20. Which of the following is defined as the use of physical or chemical means to remove, inactivate, or destroy blood-borne pathogens from a surface or item? 20.____
    A. Cleaning
    B. Disinfection
    C. Sterilization
    D. Decontamination

21. The term _____ refers to microorganisms on contaminated items. 21.____
    A. bioburden   B. biohazard   C. biocleansing   D. biotasking

22. What is the appropriate number of air exchanges in the decontamination area? 22.____
    A. 4   B. 8   C. 10   D. 12

23. The ventilation system in the decontamination area must be maintained at _____ pressure. 23.____
    A. negative   B. positive   C. neutral   D. zero

24. What is the appropriate pH level for a neutral solution? 24.____
    A. 5   B. 7   C. 9   D. 11

25. Which solution should NEVER be used to remove gross soil from instruments? 25.____
    A. Alcohol
    B. Sterile water
    C. Distilled water
    D. Saline Solution

KEY (CORRECT ANSWERS)

1.	D	11.	B
2.	B	12.	A
3.	B	13.	D
4.	C	14.	A
5.	D	15.	B
6.	D	16.	C
7.	B	17.	C
8.	B	18.	B
9.	C	19.	C
10.	D	20.	D

21.	A
22.	C
23.	A
24.	B
25.	D

EXAMINATION SECTION
TEST 1

DIRECTIONS: Each question or incomplete statement is followed by several suggested answers or completions. Select the one that BEST answers the question or completes the statement. *PRINT THE LETTER OF THE CORRECT ANSWER IN THE SPACE AT THE RIGHT.*

1. What is the MOST efficient type of dry heat sterilizer? 1.____
   A. Mechanical convection sterilizer
   B. Gravity convection sterilizer
   C. Dynamic air removal sterilizer
   D. Special purpose dry heat oven

2. What does the term *superheated steam* refer to? 2.____
   A. Moist steam at sea level
   B. Type of steam necessary for high temperature sterilization
   C. Dry steam
   D. Steam that has chemicals added in order to increase temperature

3. What would be the recommended exposure time for a dry heat sterilization load that was run at an exposure temperature of 320°F (160°C)? 3.____
   A. 1 hour   B. 1.5 hours   C. 2 hours   D. 2.5 hours

4. Where should items with solid bottoms be located when loading a steam sterilizer? 4.____
   A. On the edge
   B. Loaded first
   C. Placed in an upright position
   D. In a wire basket

5. _____ tests use live bacterial spores to challenge the efficacy of the sterilization process and provide a direct measure of lethality. 5.____
   A. Chemical indicator
   B. Biological
   C. Chemical integrator
   D. Ampulization

6. What must be done in order to elevate the temperature of a steam sterilizer? 6.____
   A. Inject boiler amines
   B. Achieve ambient pressure
   C. Decrease steam pressure
   D. Increase steam pressure

7. What is the consequence of having an object with a high bioburden? 7.____
   A. More difficult to sterilize
   B. Will take less time to sterilize
   C. Need to load more biological tests
   D. Will take longer to cool after sterilization

8. Which statement is TRUE regarding paper/plastic sterilization pouches? 8.____
   A. Should only be used for dry heat sterilization processes
   B. Should not be placed inside wrapped sets or containers
   C. Are not suitable for steam sterilization processes
   D. Are used to package wood and cork products for sterilization

9. How frequently should the strainer of a sterilizer be removed and cleaned?
   A. When the machine gauge indicates cleaning is necessary
   B. Daily
   C. Weekly
   D. Monthly

10. What bacterial spore is used for testing steam sterilizers?
    A. Geobacillus stearothermophilus
    B. Bacillus atrophaeus
    C. Pseudomonas aeruginosa
    D. Bacillus subtillus

11. What sterilization quality assurance measurements are designed to provided a written record of sterilizer cycle activity?
    A. Bowie Dick tests
    B. Mechanical recording charts/printouts
    C. Biological tests
    D. Chemical integrators

12. What statement is TRUE regarding chemical indicators?
    A. They provide a visual indication that an item was exposed to a sterilization process
    B. They prove that an item is sterile
    C. They provide information about bacterial spore kill within the sterilizer
    D. They prove that the sterilizer did not damage heat sensitive items

13. Which of the following refers to the amount of time required to kill 90% of the microorganisms present on an object?
    A. Exposure time
    B. D-value
    C. Time-weighted average
    D. Sterilization cycle

14. What do instrument washer sterilizers provide?
    A. Dry heat sterilization
    B. Terminal sterilization
    C. Flash sterilization for immediate patient use
    D. A decontamination process

15. Which of the following is TRUE when a sterilizer has successfully killed all the bacterial spores in a biological test?
    A. It is called a positive test.
    B. It is called a negative test.
    C. An alarm will sound at the completion of the cycle.
    D. It is taken out of service until it is repaired.

16. Where should Bowie-Dick tests be performed?
    A. Washer/sterilizers
    B. Downward displacement sterilizers
    C. Ethylene oxide sterilizers
    D. Dynamic air removal steam sterilizers

17. Where would information about load specific load contents be obtained in the event of a load recall?
    A. The procedure manual
    B. The sterilization log
    C. The Central Service Supervisor
    D. The Hospital Safety Director

18. How often should sterilizer recording charts and/or printouts be checked?
    A. Hourly
    B. During and at the end of each cycle
    C. Every shift
    D. Every 24 hours

19. What are the two most common temperatures used in steam sterilization?
    A. 320° and 350° - 355°F
    B. 250° and 270° - 275°F
    C. 120° and 140°F
    D. 100° and 130°F

20. Impregnated gauze strips may be sterilized through the use of _____ sterilization.
    A. dry heat
    B. ethylene oxide
    C. steam
    D. hydrogen peroxide gas plasma

21. Which of the following is an absorbent material that allows for air removal, steam penetration, and facilitates air drying?
    A. Sterile gauze
    B. Wicking material
    C. Surgical drapes
    D. Paper towels

22. What is the point of use process by which unwrapped instruments are sterilized for immediate use when an emergency situation arises?
    A. High temperature sterilization
    B. Low temperature sterilization
    C. Flash sterilization
    D. Steam sterilization

23. Which of the following is a liquid oxidizing agent that is an effective biocide at low temperatures and is used in a sterilization system that processes immersible instruments for immediate use?
    A. Peracetic acid
    B. Hydrogen peroxide
    C. Ethylene oxide
    D. Sulfuric acid

24. What is the MOST commonly used method of sterilization used in healthcare facilities?
    A. Flash sterilization
    B. Steam sterilization
    C. Ethylene oxide sterilization
    D. Hydrogen peroxide gas plasma sterilization

25. What type of steam sterilizer is used for sterilizing liquids?
    A. Mechanical convection sterilizer
    B. Gravity air displacement sterilizer
    C. Dynamic air removal sterilizer
    D. Special purpose dry heat oven

KEY (CORRECT ANSWERS)

1.	A		11.	B
2.	C		12.	A
3.	C		13.	B
4.	A		14.	D
5.	B		15.	B
6.	D		16.	D
7.	A		17.	B
8.	B		18.	B
9.	B		19.	B
10.	A		20.	A

21. B
22. C
23. A
24. B
25. B

TEST 2

DIRECTIONS: Each question or incomplete statement is followed by several suggested answers or completions. Select the one that BEST answers the question or completes the statement. *PRINT THE LETTER OF THE CORRECT ANSWER IN THE SPACE AT THE RIGHT.*

1. _____ sterilization is the process of sterilizing an item that is packaged?
    A. Steam
    B. Flash
    C. Terminal
    D. Low temperature

    1.____

2. Which of the following is a prion disease that demands that instruments be processed differently than standard protocols?
    A. Hepatitis C
    B. Creutzfeldt-Jakob Disease
    C. HIV
    D. Crohn's Disease

    2.____

3. The process by which a device is actively subjected to moving air to facilitate the removal of ethylene oxide gas is known as
    A. ventilation
    B. oxidation
    C. aeration
    D. detoxification

    3.____

4. Which of the following is a compound in which chlorine is combined with another element or radical such as a salt or hydrochloric acid?
    A. Chloride
    B. Chlorite
    C. Chlorate
    D. Chlorine

    4.____

5. What is defined as the measurement of the ability of water to carry an electrical current?
    A. Electricity
    B. Conductivity
    C. Excitability
    D. Permeability

    5.____

6. Which of the following is defined as the diffusion of water through a semi-permeable membrane to eliminate impurities in the water?
    A. Osmosis
    B. Reverse osmosis
    C. Hydrosis
    D. Meiosis

    6.____

7. A liquid solution having the sediment or solids stirred up to appear as a cloudy silicate from a mineral derived from a silica such as quartz, sand or opal is defined as
    A. liquidity
    B. turbidity
    C. solubility
    D. separability

    7.____

8. Which is defined as the unit of measure that measures the amount of resistance to an electrical current?
    A. Volts
    B. Joules
    C. Watts
    D. Ohms

    8.____

9. Which of the following is a solution to remove white, hard-to-remove, substances that sometimes appears on sinks and equipment?
    A. Deionizers
    B. Desiccants
    C. Descales
    D. Decontaminants

    9.____

10. _____ tests are used to evaluate the efficacy of an air removal system of a steam sterilizer.
    A. Biological
    B. Chemical
    C. Bowie-Dick
    D. Leak

    10.____

11. A(n) _____ trap is the portion of a steam sterilizer that measures steam temperature and automatically controls the flow of air and condensate from the sterilizer chamber.
    A. thermostatic   B. chemostatic   C. biostatic   D. electrostatic

12. Steam sterilization heats items within the load using a heat transfer process called
    A. conduction   B. ventilation   C. convection   D. dilution

13. Dry heat sterilization heats items within the load using a heat transfer process called
    A. conduction   B. ventilation   C. convection   D. dilution

14. Which of the following is the NEWEST low temperature sterilization process?
    A. Ethylene oxide gas
    B. Hydrogen peroxide
    C. Peracetic acid
    D. Ozone

15. Which method of low temperature sterilization has been in use since the 1960s?
    A. Ethylene oxide gas
    B. Hydrogen peroxide
    C. Peracetic acid
    D. Ozone

16. What is the proper cycle time for items sterilized using hydrogen peroxide gas plasma?
    A. Less than 1 hour
    B. 1 hour
    C. 2 hours
    D. 4 hours

17. What is the proper cycle time for items using ozone sterilization?
    A. 2 hours   B. 4 hours   C. 6 hours   D. 8 hours

18. What is the proper 140°F aeration time for items sterilized with ethylene oxide?
    A. 2 hours   B. 4 hours   C. 6 hours   D. 8 hours

19. What is the bacterial spore used to test ethylene oxide sterilization cycles?
    A. Geobacillus stearothermophilus
    B. Bacillus atrophaeus
    C. Pseudomonas aeruginosa
    D. Bacillus subtillus

20. What is the appropriate cycle time for items sterilized using ethylene oxide sterilization?
    A. 6 hours   B. 8 hours   C. 10 hours   D. 12+ hours

21. Which agency has exposure standards for chemical sterilants?
    A. Food and Drug Administration
    B. Occupational Health and Safety Administration
    C. Centers for Disease Control and Prevention
    D. National Institute of Health

22. Which agency requires that sterilants be rigorously tested prior to being marketed?
    A. Food and Drug Administration
    B. Occupational Health and Safety Administration
    C. Centers for Disease Control and Prevention
    D. National Institute of Health

23. Large instruments in a set should be evenly distributed to prevent the formation of which of the following?
    A. Condensation   B. Silicates   C. Bacteria   D. Prions

24. Which agency is responsible for regulating environmental disinfectants?
    A. Food and Drug Administration
    B. Occupational Health and Safety Administration
    C. Centers for Disease Control and Prevention
    D. Environmental Protection Agency

25. Medical-grade Kraft paper CANNOT be used with which of the following sterilization processes?
    A. Low temperature   B. Low temperature gas plasma
    C. Ethylene oxide   D. Ozone

KEY (CORRECT ANSWERS)

1.	C	11.	A
2.	B	12.	C
3.	C	13.	A
4.	A	14.	D
5.	B	15.	A
6.	B	16.	A
7.	B	17.	B
8.	D	18.	D
9.	C	19.	B
10.	C	20.	D

21.	B
22.	A
23.	A
24.	D
25.	B

TEST 3

DIRECTIONS: Each question or incomplete statement is followed by several suggested answers or completions. Select the one that BEST answers the question or completes the statement. *PRINT THE LETTER OF THE CORRECT ANSWER IN THE SPACE AT THE RIGHT.*

1. How are items that have a large dollar value but are used infrequently classified during cycle counts?
   A. Class A   B. Class B   C. Class C   D. Class D

   1._____

2. For non-tabletop steam sterilizes, where is the steam generated?
   A. Condenser   B. Generator   C. Boiler   D. Refractor

   2._____

3. What type of indicator is autoclave tape considered?
   A. Class 1   B. Class 2   C. Class 4   D. Class 5

   3._____

4. Which part of the steam sterilizer produces heat inside the chamber to prevent condensation from forming on the chamber walls?
   A. Boiler   B. Jacket   C. Generator   D. Condenser

   4._____

5. What process can minimize the need for frequent instrument reprocessing?
   A. Proper stock rotation
   B. Proper handling of materials
   C. Proper use by operating room staff
   D. Proper method of sterilization

   5._____

6. What is the coldest part of the sterilizer?
   A. Boiler   B. Jacket   C. Drain line   D. Condenser

   6._____

7. Gradual heating of packs occurs during which phase of the steam sterilization cycle?
   A. Pre-heating   B. Cooling   C. Conditioning   D. Drying

   7._____

8. What is the MOST important thing to remember when double-peel pouching?
   A. The outer pouch must completely encompass the inner pouch.
   B. The inner pouch must lay flat inside the outer pouch.
   C. The outer pouch must be twice as large as the inner pouch.
   D. The inner pouch must not touch the outer pouch.

   8._____

9. Which of the following BEST describes a minimum exposure time, temperature, and pressure for pre-vacuum steam sterilization of wrapped items?
   A. 4 minutes at 270°F and 28-30 pounds per square inch
   B. 3 minutes at 270°F and 38-40 pounds per square inch
   C. 15 minutes at 250°F and 28-30 pounds per square inch
   D. 30 minutes at 250°F and 28-40 pounds per square inch

   9._____

10. Incoming saturated steam should be within what range of dryness?
    A. 5% - 6%   B. 10% - 12%   C. 51% - 55%   D. 97% - 100%

    10._____

11. What will result if there is a failure to remove all air from a package within a steam sterilizer?
    A. Excess steam penetration
    B. Poor steam penetration
    C. Corrosion of instruments
    D. Decreased bioburden

    11.____

12. Steam is exhausted from the sterilizer through which of the following?
    A. Boiler
    B. Generator
    C. Jacket
    D. Chamber drain line

    12.____

13. For what reason must textile packs be placed on their sides for sterilization?
    A. To ensure they fit properly in the sterilizer
    B. To avoid corrosion of instruments
    C. To facilitate proper air removal and steam penetration
    D. To be able to sterilize the maximum number of instruments simultaneously

    13.____

14. What is the MOST unique feature of integrating a chemical indicator to the sterilization process?
    A. It performs parallel to biological indicators.
    B. It performs parallel to Bowie-Dick tests.
    C. It makes documentation/record keeping easier.
    D. It ensures highest degree of sterilization.

    14.____

15. What process does ethylene oxide use to kill microorganisms?
    A. Acidation   B. Oxidation   C. Alkylation   D. Hydration

    15.____

16. What is the nominal concentration of hydrogen peroxide in a low-temperature gas plasma sterilizer?
    A. 49%   B. 59%   C. 69%   D. 79%

    16.____

17. When should rigid sterilization containers be biologically tested?
    A. Prior to purchasing
    B. Prior to use
    C. Prior to initial cleaning
    D. Prior to entrance to the facility

    17.____

18. Which of the following is NOT a factor affecting the dry time of a steam sterilizer?
    A. Type of packaging
    B. Weight of sets
    C. Selected sterilization time
    D. Configuration of the load

    18.____

19. Ethylene oxide is regulated by all of the following agencies EXCEPT
    A. Occupational Health and Safety Administration
    B. Environmental Protection Agency
    C. Food and Drug Administration
    D. Centers for Disease Control and Prevention

    19.____

20. Effective sterilization begins with which of the following?
    A. Selection of proper sterilization method
    B. Thorough cleaning
    C. Proper use of instruments by operating room staff
    D. Selection of proper detergent

21. An exhaust hood over the ethylene oxide sterilizer is an example of which of the following?
    A. Engineering control
    B. Biological control
    C. Chemical control
    D. Environmental control

22. Which of the following is the CORRECT incubation temperature range for biological indicators used in steam sterilization?
    A. 131°F - 140°F
    B. 140°F - 183°F
    C. 250°F - 275°F
    D. 270°F - 275°F

23. A chemical indicator responding to two or more critical parameters belongs to which class?
    A. 2
    B. 3
    C. 4
    D. 6

24. How should the pouches be placed when placing paper-plastic pouches in a sterilizer?
    A. Paper facing paper in a basket
    B. Plastic facing plastic in a basket
    C. Paper facing plastic in a basket
    D. Face down in a basket

25. _____ is the MOST effective method of killing microbes?
    A. Ethylene oxide sterilization
    B. Autoclaving
    C. Ozone sterilization
    D. Gas plasma sterilization

KEY (CORRECT ANSWERS)

1. A
2. C
3. A
4. B
5. A

6. C
7. C
8. B
9. A
10. D

11. B
12. D
13. C
14. A
15. C

16. B
17. A
18. C
19. D
20. B

21. A
22. A
23. C
24. C
25. B

TEST 4

DIRECTIONS: Each question or incomplete statement is followed by several suggested answers or completions. Select the one that BEST answers the question or completes the statement. *PRINT THE LETTER OF THE CORRECT ANSWER IN THE SPACE AT THE RIGHT.*

1. Vials or strips, also known as spore tests, that contain harmless bacterial spores and are used to assess the function of a sterilizer are known as
    A. chemical indicators
    B. biological indicators
    C. Bowie-Dick test
    D. environmental indicators

    1.____

2. What is the piece of equipment that is used for sterilization through the use of moist heat under pressure?
    A. Gas plasma sterilizer
    B. Ozone sterilizer
    C. Ethylene oxide sterilizer
    D. Autoclave

    2.____

3. Which of the following is a piece of equipment that is used for sterilization through the use of hot formaldehyde vapors under pressure?
    A. Autoclave
    B. Chemical vapor sterilizer
    C. Dry heat sterilizer
    D. Ozone sterilizer

    3.____

4. A _____ instrument is an instrument to penetrate soft tissue or bone.
    A. non-critical   B. semi-critical   C. critical   D. hyper-critical

    4.____

5. A _____ instrument is an instrument that comes into contact with oral tissues but do not penetrate soft tissue or bone.
    A. non-critical   B. semi-critical   C. critical   D. hyper-critical

    5.____

6. A _____ instrument is an instrument that only comes into contact with the skin.
    A. non-critical   B. semi-critical   C. critical   D. hyper-critical

    6.____

7. Which of the following is a piece of equipment used for sterilization by means of heated air?
    A. Autoclave
    B. Chemical vapor sterilizer
    C. Dry heat sterilizer
    D. ozone sterilizer

    7.____\

8. Tapes, strips, and tabs with heat-sensitive chemicals that change color when exposed to certain temperatures are referred to as _____ indicators.
    A. biological
    B. environmental
    C. single parameter
    D. multi-parameter

    8.____

9. An indicator that reacts to time, temperature, and the presence of steam is referred to as _____ indicators.
    A. biological
    B. environmental
    C. single parameter
    D. multi-parameter

    9.____

10. In what should instruments be placed if they cannot be processed immediately?
    A. Saline solution   B. Holding solution
    C. Sterile water   D. Distilled water

11. Use of _____ can prevent the rusting of an instrument.
    A. sterilants   B. lubricants   C. dessicants   D. disinfectants

12. Where should a process indicator be placed?
    A. Outside the package   B. Inside the package
    C. On the surface of the instrument D. Outside the sterilizer

13. Where should a process integrator be placed?
    A. Outside the package   B. Inside the package
    C. On the surface of the instrument D. Outside the sterilizer

14. What is the disadvantage to flash sterilization?
    A. Instruments will rust
    B. Cannot assess bioburden
    C. Inability to wrap items
    D. Don't know the condition of instruments prior to sterilization

15. What is the advantage of chemical vapor sterilization?
    A. Instruments will not rust.
    B. Instruments can be wrapped
    C. Bioburden easily assessed
    D. Most trustworthy form of sterilization

16. What are the two types of dry heat sterilization?
    A. Trapped air and cycled air   B. Static air and forced air
    C. Cycled air and static air   D. Forced air and trapped air

17. With what should you rinse instruments that have been processed in a liquid chemical sterilant?
    A. Alcohol   B. Acetone
    C. Distilled water   D. Sterile water

18. What type of sterilization is appropriate for high-speed hand pieces?
    A. Steam and chemical vapor   B. Ozone and ethylene oxide
    C. Hydrogen peroxide and ozone   D. Chemical vapor and ozone

19. High-speed hand pieces should be flushed with _____ to prepare them for sterilization.
    A. alcohol   B. water
    C. saline   D. acetone

20. What is the preferred method of sterilization for instruments with complex parts, fiber-optics, or camera?
    A. Dry heat sterilization   B. Chemical sterilization
    C. Low temperature sterilization   D. Autoclaving

21. Chemical sterilization qualification of a device requires all of the following EXCEPT _____ testing.
    A. environmental
    B. microbiological
    C. engineering
    D. toxicological

22. Integrating indicators that react to all critical variables with the stated values having been generated to be equivalent to, or exceed, the performance requirements should be assigned to Class
    A. 2
    B. 3
    C. 4
    D. 5

23. What does a negative result for a biological indicator indicate?
    A. Proper sterilization has been met.
    B. Proper sterilization has not been met.
    C. Proper conditions for sterilization have been met.
    D. Proper conditions for sterilization have not been met.

24. Biological indicators should be run with every implant with the exception of which of the following?
    A. Autoclaving
    B. Ethylene oxide
    C. Dry heat
    D. High temperature

25. When moisture comes into contact with ethylene oxide, it forms _____, which is toxic to humans.
    A. ethylene glycol
    B. ethyl alcohol
    C. ethylbenzene
    D. propionaldehyde

KEY (CORRECT ANSWERS)

1.	B		11.	B
2.	D		12.	A
3.	B		13.	B
4.	C		14.	C
5.	B		15.	A
6.	A		16.	B
7.	C		17.	D
8.	C		18.	A
9.	D		19.	B
10.	B		20.	C

21. A
22. D
23. C
24. B
25. A

EXAMINATION SECTION
TEST 1

DIRECTIONS: Each question or incomplete statement is followed by several suggested answers or completions. Select the one that BEST answers the question or completes the statement. *PRINT THE LETTER OF THE CORRECT ANSWER IN THE SPACE AT THE RIGHT.*

1. Kerrison Laminectomy Rongeurs should be tested using which of the following? 1.____
   A. Tissue paper
   B. Index card
   C. Rubber testing material
   D. Plastic dowel rod

2. Which of the following is NOT an acceptable form of instrument marking? 2.____
   A. Laser-etching
   B. Acid-based etching
   C. Heat-infused nylon
   D. Electric etching

3. Scissors with tungsten carbide cutting edges are usually identified by what color? 3.____
   A. Gold
   B. Black
   C. Silver
   D. Red

4. What is the purpose of a suction stylet? 4.____
   A. Facilitate the sterilization process
   B. Provide a measuring guide for the surgeon
   C. Unclog the suction during surgery
   D. Facilitate blood flow during surgical procedures

5. Endoscopes are often processed in a mechanical unit known as 5.____
   A. ultrasonic cleaner
   B. washer-decontaminator
   C. automatic endoscope reprocessor
   D. flush-pulse endoscope reprocessor

6. What is the FIRST step to inspect the insulation of a laparascopic instrument? 6.____
   A. Check the collar at the distal tip
   B. Attempt to slide the insulation back
   C. Check the handle for chipping or cracking
   D. Check the collar at the proximal tip

7. Which of the following statements are TRUE regarding endoscopes? 7.____
   A. Not all endoscopes can be processed in an automatic endoscopic reprocessor.
   B. Ultrasonic cleaning is the process of choice for endoscopes.
   C. All endoscopes should be steam sterilized.
   D. Flexible endoscopes are not easily damaged.

8. What should be the FIRST step when processing flexible endoscopes? 8.____
   A. High level sterilization
   B. Manual cleaning
   C. Leak testing
   D. Drying

9. Which endoscope would be dispensed for a procedure that required visualization of the lower part of the large intestine?
   A. Colonoscope
   B. Sigmoidoscope
   C. Ureteroscope
   D. Gastroscope

10. What is the purpose of using a decontamination battery or cord when cleaning powered surgical instruments?
    A. To keep fluid from entering the unit
    B. To keep functioning batteries and cords clean
    C. To prevent electrical shock
    D. To test the unit while cleaning

11. Who should provide information regarding cleaning processes for endoscopes?
    A. Hospital policies
    B. Endoscope manufacturer
    C. Society of Gastroenterology Nurses and Associates
    D. Association for Professionals in Infection Control and Epidemiology

12. Where should electronic testing of laparoscopic insulation be performed?
    A. In the contamination area prior to cleaning
    B. In the operating room at the end of the procedure
    C. At the factory or onsite repair unit
    D. In the clean assembly area prior to set assembly

13. What substance should be used to thoroughly rinse all traces of disinfectant from the channels of an endoscope?
    A. Filtered water
    B. Forced air
    C. Water containing approved sterilant
    D. Heated gluteraldehyde

14. Which of the following statements is TRUE regarding loaner instruments?
    A. They should be decontaminated prior to use.
    B. They should never be used.
    C. They should be sterilized using a low temperature process.
    D. They should be decontaminated only if they appear to be soiled.

15. Which of the following common items of patient care equipment limits the development of deep vein thrombosis and peripheral edema in immobile patients?
    A. Respirator
    B. Intermittent suction device
    C. Sequential compression unit
    D. Defibrillator

16. Where is patient care equipment typically stored?
    A. On patient units
    B. In sterile storage areas
    C. In the Central Service Department
    D. In the Biomedical Engineering Department

17. When patient equipment enters a healthcare facility, who has the responsibility of checking it prior to patient use?
    A. Biomedical Technician
    B. Central Service Technician
    C. Central Service Director
    D. Infection Control Committee Member

18. Which of the following is TRUE regarding tracking of patient care equipment?
    A. Tracking patient care equipment can prevent equipment shortages.
    B. Tracking of patient care equipment requires a computer.
    C. Patient care equipment should only be tracked if it has a value in excess of an amount specified by the facility.
    D. Patient care equipment should only be tracked if its usage will be charged to the patients.

19. When should equipment be inspected for obvious hazards such as cracked or frayed electrical cords?
    A. Prior to patient use
    B. During preventative maintenance activities
    C. When there are complaints from user department personnel
    D. When the equipment is being cleaned

20. Which piece of legislation requires that the healthcare facility report malfunctions of medical devices that have contributed to patient injury, illness and/or death to the manufacturer and the FDA?
    A. Safe Medical Devices Act
    B. FDA Equipment Notification Act
    C. EPA Patient Security Act
    D. OSHA Patient Safety Act

21. All patient care equipment that is dispensed for use must be considered _____ and handled as such regardless of its appearance.
    A. clean   B. sterile   C. visibly soiled   D. contaminated

22. Which hospital department employs technicians that perform safety inspections and functional tests on equipment?
    A. Maintenance
    B. Biomedical Engineering
    C. Materials Management
    D. Infection Control

23. Which agency requires preventative maintenance standards be established for medical equipment?
    A. Joint Commission
    B. Occupational Safety and Health Administration
    C. Association of PeriOperative Registered Nurses
    D. Association for the Advancement of Medical Instrumentation

24. Which of the following statements is TRUE regarding disposable components such as pads and tubing on patient care equipment?
They such be
    A. discarded at point of use
    B. discarded during preventative maintenance
    C. reprocessed for re-use
    D. removed in the Biomedical Engineering Department

24.____

25. What should occur if an equipment malfunction causes harm to patients?
Equipment should be
    A. discarded immediately
    B. sequestered for inspection by OSHA personnel
    C. sent to the manufacturer for repairs
    D. returned immediately to the Biomedical Department

25.____

KEY (CORRECT ANSWERS)

1.	B		11.	B
2.	D		12.	D
3.	A		13.	A
4.	C		14.	A
5.	C		15.	C
6.	A		16.	D
7.	A		17.	A
8.	C		18.	B
9.	B		19.	D
10.	A		20.	D

21. D
22. C
23. B
24. A
25. D

TEST 2

DIRECTIONS: Each question or incomplete statement is followed by several suggested answers or completions. Select the one that BEST answers the question or completes the statement. *PRINT THE LETTER OF THE CORRECT ANSWER IN THE SPACE AT THE RIGHT.*

1. What is the difference between equipment leasing and equipment rental? 1.____
   A. Equipment leasing is an operating expense; equipment rental does not have cost implications.
   B. Leasing involves purchase; rental does not require ownership.
   C. Equipment rental is usually done on a shorter-term basis than equipment leasing.
   D. Equipment leasing involves the most expensive equipment; equipment rental involves less expensive equipment.

2. In what condition should patient care equipment be stored? 2.____
   A. Ready to clean   B. Ready to inspect
   C. Ready to sterilize   D. Ready to use

3. Which of the following statements is TRUE regarding preventative maintenance for patient care equipment? 3.____
   A. It is designed to identify potential problems before they occur.
   B. It is designed to be performed when a piece of equipment injures a patient.
   C. It is performed when user unit notices a problem.
   D. It is performed by Central Service prior to the equipment being dispensed.

4. What can result from laparoscopic instrument insulation failure? 4.____
   A. Cuts   B. Scrapes   C. Burns   D. Bruises

5. The purpose of a decontamination battery is to protect from _____ invasion. 5.____
   A. dust   B. fluid   C. prion   D. bacterial

6. Which of the following is NOT an appropriate power source for powered surgical instruments? 6.____
   A. Air   B. Battery   C. Electricity   D. Solar

7. What type of endoscope allows for visual inspection of the upper digestive tract? 7.____
   A. Gastroscope   B. Bronchoscope
   C. Sigmoidoscope   D. Cystoscope

8. What type of endoscope allows for visual inspection of the urethra and the bladder? 8.____
   A. Sigmoidoscope   B. Cystoscope
   C. Bronchoscope   D. Colonoscope

9. What type of endoscope allows for visualization of the tracheobronchial tree?
   A. Cystoscope   B. Sigmoidoscope
   C. Gastroscope   D. Broncoscope

10. What type of endoscope allows for visualization of the entire large intestine?
    A. Colonoscope   B. Gastroscope
    C. Sigmoidoscope   D. Cystoscope

11. What powered surgical instrument is used for driving very small wires through bone?
    A. Sternal saw   B. Cebatome   C. Dermatome   D. Micro Drill

12. What powered surgical instrument would be used for open heart surgery?
    A. Dermabrader   B. Sternal saw   C. Cebatome   D. Micro Drill

13. What powered surgical instrument is used to remove cement?
    A. Dermatome   B. Cebatome   C. Dental Drill   D. Micro Drill

14. What powered surgical instrument would be used to harvest skin grafts and reshape skin surfaces?
    A. Dermatome   B. Cebatome   C. Sternal Saw   D. Micro Drill

15. Which piece of equipment would be used to perform specific cutting actions such as reciprocating or oscillating?
    A. Scissors   B. Forceps   C. Saw   D. Retractors

16. Which surgical instrument would be used to cut, incise, or dissect tissue?
    A. Retractors   B. Scissors   C. Saw   D. Forceps

17. Prolonged exposure to which common operating room substance can result in damage to instruments?
    A. Betadine   B. Alcohol
    C. Deionized water   D. Saline solution

18. Which of the following surgical instruments would be used to grasp?
    A. Forceps   B. Retractors   C. Cebatome   D. Dermatone

19. What is the part of a ring-handled instrument where the two parts meet and pivot?
    A. Box lock   B. Joint lock   C. Hinge lock   D. Bolt lock

20. Tissue forceps have _____ and dressing forceps have _____.
    A. serrations; teeth   B. teeth; serrations
    C. rubber tips; steel tips   D. steel tips; rubber tips

21. Which type of stainless steel, also known as 400 series stainless steel, can be heat-hardened and used for the manufacturing of surgical instruments?
    A. Ferritic stainless steel   B. Austenitic stainless steel
    C. Martensitic stainless steel   D. Precipitation hardened steel

22. What piece of surgical equipment is a self-retaining retractor? 22.____
    A. Rongeurs B. Gelpi C. Ratchet D. Cannulas

23. Which part of a ring-handled instrument locks the handles in place? 23.____
    A. Box lock B. Ratchet C. Joint lock D. Gelpi

24. What piece of surgical equipment is used to cut away bone and tissue? 24.____
    A. Saw B. Scissors C. Rongeurs D. Forceps

25. What is the chemical process that is applied during the manufacturing of surgical instruments that provides a corrosion-resistant finish by forming a thin, transparent oxide film? 25.____
    A. Sterilization B. Cavitation
    C. Passivation D. Decontamination

KEY (CORRECT ANSWERS)

1.	B	11.	D
2.	D	12.	B
3.	A	13.	B
4.	C	14.	A
5.	B	15.	C
6.	D	16.	B
7.	A	17.	D
8.	B	18.	A
9.	D	19.	A
10.	A	20.	B

21. C
22. B
23. B
24. C
25. C

TEST 3

DIRECTIONS: Each question or incomplete statement is followed by several suggested answers or completions. Select the one that BEST answers the question or completes the statement. *PRINT THE LETTER OF THE CORRECT ANSWER IN THE SPACE AT THE RIGHT.*

1. Which of the following is a surgical instrument with a hollow barrel through the center?
   A. Cannulas   B. Retractors   C. Rongeurs   D. Gelpi

   1.____

2. Which of the following is the internal path through a needle, tube, or surgical instrument?
   A. Cannulas   B. Lumen   C. Catheter   D. Tunnel

   2.____

3. What is the MOST corrosion-resistant form of stainless steel?
   A. Austenitic stainless steels
   B. Ferritic stainless steels
   C. Precipitation hardened stainless steels
   D. Martensitic stainless steels

   3.____

4. What is the proper method for cleaning fiber-optic light cables?
   A. In the autoclave
   B. Soft cloth and detergent
   C. Vigorous scraping
   D. Hydrogen peroxide and rinsed with distilled water

   4.____

5. The mechanical action in the ultra cleaning process that uses sound waves and imploding bubbles is called
   A. passivation   B. cavitation
   C. sterilization   D. decontamination

   5.____

6. Which piece of equipment is an example of a flexible endoscope?
   A. Cystoscope   B. Cavitation
   C. Arthroscope   D. Resectoscope

   6.____

7. Which piece of equipment is used to regulate body temperature?
   A. Sequential compression device   B. Cebatome
   C. Dermatome   D. Hypo/Hyperthermia machine

   7.____

8. _____ compression devices are used to prevent the formation of blood clots.
   A. Sequential   B. Standardized
   C. Sterilized   D. Subcutaneous

   8.____

9. What is the appropriate grade of stainless steel used to manufacture osteotomes?
   A. 200 Grade   B. 300 Grade   C. 400 Grade   D. 500 Grade

   9.____

10. For manual lubrication, surgical instruments should be placed in a lubricant solution and then
    A. sterilized
    B. autoclaved
    C. wiped clean
    D. room air-dried

11. It is appropriate to use dissecting scissors to cut
    A. dressings   B. bone   C. wire   D. tissue

12. The purpose of the tungsten carbine insert on a needle holder is to _____ the suture needle better.
    A. guide   B. place   C. maneuver   D. hold

13. What piece of equipment is used to artificially stimulate the venous plantar plexus in order to increase circulation of bed-ridden patients?
    A. Defibrillator
    B. Foot pump
    C. Sequential pressure device
    D. Pacemaker

14. Which piece of equipment applies a brief electroshock to restore the rhythm of the heart?
    A. Pacemaker   B. Defibrillator   C. Metabolizer   D. Retractor

15. An emergency eyewash station must be which of the following?
    A. Completely automated
    B. Hands-on operated
    C. Hands-free operated
    D. Manually operated

16. Which organization has established standards for the effective processing of flexible endoscopes?
    A. Society of Gastroenterology Nurses and Associates
    B. Association for Professionals in Infection Control and Epidemiology
    C. Association of PeriOperative Registered Nurses
    D. Association for the Advancement of Medical Instrumentation

17. Instruments with lumens should be soaked in what position?
    A. Horizontal
    B. Vertical
    C. At a 30° angle
    D. At a 45° angle

18. Automatic washers clean using spray-force action called
    A. containment
    B. impalement
    C. impingement
    D. enforcement

19. Which piece of equipment allows the patient to self-administer pain medication?
    A. Foot pump
    B. Sequential pressure device
    C. Heart pump
    D. Patient controlled analgesia pump

20. Which of the following statements is TRUE regarding powered surgical instruments?
    A. Hoses that attach to pneumatic-powered instruments should not be sterilized.
    B. Cables should be disconnected from the handpiece during processing.
    C. Powered surgical instruments should be completely disassembled prior to processing.
    D. It is important that fluid does not enter the cable or handpiece during processing.

21. The decision to sterilize or high-level disinfect an endoscope is based according to which classification system?
    A. Nightingale
    B. Spaulding
    C. Schrodinger
    D. Federal Medical Device

22. What type of fire extinguisher is appropriate to be used on flammable objects?
    A. Type A   B. Type B   C. Type C   D. Type D

23. Microgrind or Supercut scissors are usually identified by what color handle?
    A. Black   B. Blue   C. Silver   D. Red

24. An ionsufflator blows what gas into the patient's abdominal cavity in order to extend the laparoscope and allow the surgeon to view the patient's internal organs?
    A. Carbon monoxide
    B. Carbon dioxide
    C. Nitric oxide
    D. Helium nitride

25. At what pressure does the insufflator blow gasses into the abdominal cavity?
    A. 5mmHg – 8 mmHg
    B. 9mmHg – 11mmHg
    C. 12mmHg – 15mmHg
    D. 16mmHg – 19mmHg

KEY (CORRECT ANSWERS)

1. A
2. B
3. A
4. B
5. B

6. B
7. D
8. A
9. C
10. D

11. D
12. D
13. B
14. B
15. C

16. A
17. B
18. C
19. D
20. A

21. B
22. B
23. A
24. B
25. C

TEST 4

DIRECTIONS: Each question or incomplete statement is followed by several suggested answers or completions. Select the one that BEST answers the question or completes the statement. *PRINT THE LETTER OF THE CORRECT ANSWER IN THE SPACE AT THE RIGHT.*

1. What do many laparoscopic instruments have to deliver electrosurgical energy to the distal end of the instrument?
    A. Insulation
    B. Tungsten carbide tips
    C. Cautery posts
    D. Defibrillators

    1.____

2. What part of a laparoscope is NOT used for access or exposure of a surgical site?
    A. Cautery post
    B. Camera
    C. Light source
    D. Insufflator

    2.____

3. Which of the following is used to transmit light in a laparoscope to the surgical site?
    A. Electricity
    B. Fiber-optic cables
    C. Microwaves
    D. Ultrasonic waves

    3.____

4. What type of light sources could be connected to the laparoscope with a cable?
    A. Helium and neon
    B. Argon and neon
    C. Halogen and xenon
    D. Argon and xenon

    4.____

5. Laparoscopic equipment that is NOT part of the sterile field is decontaminated as part of what process?
    A. Room cleaning
    B. Instrument cleaning
    C. Sterilization
    D. Ionization

    5.____

6. After they are disassembled, what should be used to wipe blood from the outer surfaces on non-immersible items?
    A. Hydrogen peroxide
    B. Sterile water
    C. Alcohol
    D. Betadine

    6.____

7. Which of the following should be used to assist cleaning of box-locks, serrations, and other crevices?
    A. Wire-bristled brush
    B. Soft-bristled brush
    C. Sterile towel
    D. Sterile gauze

    7.____

8. Instruments should be kept under the solution while cleaning to avoid the creation of
    A. contaminants
    B. condensation
    C. aerosols
    D. prions

    8.____

9. Because it is inserted blindly, which part of the laparoscope can cause injuries to blood vessels and organs if it is inserted too far?
   A. Trocar
   B. Camera
   C. Fiber-optic cables
   D. Insufflator

10. The _____ optic surface is NOT one of the optical areas to clean on a laparoscope.
    A. internal   B. distal   C. fiber   D. proximal

11. What is the minimum amount of time that is required for flushing the internal channel of a laparoscope to allow for adequate removal of organic debris?
    A. 10 seconds   B. 20 seconds   C. 30 seconds   D. 40 seconds

12. What may be an indication that some of the fibers are broken in a laparoscope?
    A. Cracked appearance
    B. Double vision
    C. Appearance of black dots
    D. Over-illumination

13. Any bare metal, where there should be insulation, can cause electrical _____ during the surgical procedure and potentially burn vital organs inside the patient but outside the view of the surgeon.
    A. arcing   B. avalanching   C. adversity   D. advancement

14. Which of the following is TRUE regarding ergonomic injuries?
    A. Not a concern for Central Service employees
    B. Are a risk factor for persons who perform repetitive or physical work
    C. Are rare in today's work environment
    D. Only occur in an office setting

15. Which of the following is TRUE regarding secondary containers of chemicals?
    A. Must be labeled with a permanent marker and must state the name of the chemical and designated storage location.
    B. There are no restrictions regarding secondary container labels.
    C. Must be labeled with a copy of the original manufacturer's label or a generic label that identifies hazard warnings and directions.
    D. Secondary containers of chemicals are forbidden in healthcare facilities.

16. What is burning in a Class C fire?
    A. Wood or paper
    B. Cloth or plastic
    C. Flammable liquid
    D. Energized electrical equipment

17. Which of the following is NOT required to ensure sharps safety?
    A. Never use your fingers to remove a blade from a scalpel.
    B. Wash all disposable sharps prior to discarding them.
    C. Separate reusable sharps in an appropriate container.
    D. Dispose all single use sharps in an appropriate container.

18. What process will help instrument identification tape adhere to the instrument? 18.____
    A. Passivation   B. Cavitation
    C. Autoclaving   D. Decontamination

19. Heart valves and pacemakers are examples of what class of medical device by the Food and Drug Administration? 19.____
    A. Class I   B. Class II   C. Class III   D. Class IV

20. Class III medical devices are classified by the Food and Drug Administration as _____ risk. 20.____
    A. no   B. low   C. intermediate   D. high

21. Failure to receive accreditation from the Joint Commission can result in the facility's loss of 21.____
    A. patients   B. privileges
    C. Medicare reimbursement   D. physicians

22. Which agency imposes very strict labeling requirements on manufacturers of chemicals used by the Central Service Department? 22.____
    A. Food and Drug Administration
    B. Environmental Protection Agency
    C. Occupational Safety and Health Administration
    D. Centers for Disease Control and Prevention

23. Which agency is responsible for administering regulations under the Clean Air Act? 23.____
    A. Environmental Protection Agency
    B. Food and Drug Administration
    C. Association of PeriOperative Registered Nurses
    D. Association for the Advancement of Medical Instrumentation

24. Which organization sets recommended practices and standards for care and processing of medical devices and systems? 24.____
    A. Association of PeriOperative Registered Nurses
    B. Association for the Advancement of Medical Instrumentation
    C. Society of Gastroenterology Nurses and Associates
    D. Association for Professionals in Infection Control and Epidemiology

25. Which of the following substances break down blood, mucous, feces, and albumin? 25.____
    A. Lipase   B. Protease enzymes
    C. Surfactant   D. Ethylene oxide

KEY (CORRECT ANSWERS)

1.	C	11.	B
2.	A	12.	C
3.	B	13.	A
4.	C	14.	B
5.	A	15.	D
6.	B	16.	D
7.	B	17.	B
8.	C	18.	C
9.	A	19.	C
10.	A	20.	D

21. C
22. B
23. A
24. B
25. B

EXAMINATION SECTION
TEST 1

DIRECTIONS: Each question or incomplete statement is followed by several suggested answers or completions. Select the one that BEST answers the question or completes the statement. *PRINT THE LETTER OF THE CORRECT ANSWER IN THE SPACE AT THE RIGHT.*

1. Which of the following is NOT considered to be a safe practice? 1.____
   A. Discard open sterile bottles.
   B. Sterile persons drape first toward themselves, then away.
   C. Sterile persons face sterile areas
   D. Sterile tables may be covered for future use.

2. What is the MINIMUM distance a nonsterile person should remain from a sterile field? 2.____
   A. 1 foot   B. 3 feet   C. 5 feet   D. 10 feet

3. Which of the following is NOT an acceptable wrapper for gas sterilization? 3.____
   A. Nylon   B. Muslin   C. Paper   D. Plastic

4. Which of the following is the only acceptable plastic that can be used for a steam sterilization wrapper? 4.____
   A. Polyethylene   B. Polypropylene
   C. Polyamide   D. Polyvinyl chloride

5. All of the following statements are true regarding muslin wrappers EXCEPT: 5.____
   A. Muslin must be laundered, even if unused, in order to rehydrate it.
   B. A 140 thread count of unbleached muslin is used for wrappers.
   C. Muslin is flexible and easy to handle.
   D. Small holes can be repaired by stitching on a patch.

6. _____ days is the MAXIMUM storage life for a muslin wrapped item in a closed cabinet. 6.____
   A. 7   B. 14   C. 21   D. 30

7. Which of the following statements is FALSE regarding the scrub procedure? 7.____
   A. It reduces microbial count.   B. It leaves an antimicrobial residue.
   C. It renders the skin aseptic.   D. It removes skin oil.

8. Which statement regarding removal of gown and gloves FAILS to meet safe criteria? 8.____
   A. Gloves are removed before the gown.
   B. The gown is pulled off inside out.
   C. The scrub nurse pulls the gloves off.
   D. The scrub uses closed-glove technique to reapply gloves.

9. Which of the following statements regarding the surgical scrub is NOT an acceptable practice?
   A. Fingernails should not extend beyond the tip of the finger.
   B. Nail polish may be worn if it is freshly applied.
   C. Staff members with cuts, abrasions, or hangnails should not scrub in.
   D. A non-oil-based hand lotion may be used to protect the skin.

10. How many pounds of pressure is required of a steam sterilizer set at 250°F?
    A. 8-10   B. 11-14   C. 15-17   D. 18-21

11. The MINIMUM exposure time for unwrapped instruments in a flash sterilizer that is set at 270°F is _____ minutes.
    A. 3   B. 5   C. 7   D. 10

12. To be sterilized effectively, a linen pack must not weigh more than _____ lbs.
    A. 5   B. 8   C. 12   D. 15

13. All of the following statements are true regarding instrument sets EXCEPT:
    A. Instruments must be placed in perforated trays.
    B. Heavy instruments are placed on the bottom
    C. All instruments must be closed.
    D. All detachable parts must be disassembled.

14. All of the following statements are true regarding steam sterilization EXCEPT:
    A. Flat packages are placed on the shelf.
    B. Small packages placed one on top of the other are criss-crossed.
    C. Basins are placed on their sides.
    D. Solutions may be autoclaved along with other items as long as they are on a shelf alone.

15. Wrapped basin sets must be sterilized by steam under a pressure of 250°F for a MINIMUM of _____ minutes.
    A. 10   B. 20   C. 30   D. 40

16. Which of the following statements is TRUE regarding the sterilization of basin sets?
    A. Basins must be separated by a porous material if they are nested.
    B. Sponges and linen may be packaged inside the basin to be sterilized.
    C. Basins are placed flat in the autoclave.
    D. Basins must always be placed on the top shelf of the autoclave in a combined load.

17. Which of the following is critical when using activated glutaraldehyde for sterilization?
    A. Items must be rinsed thoroughly in sterile water prior to use.
    B. Solution must be heated in order to be effective.
    C. Items must be thoroughly moistened prior to placement in the solution.
    D. Items must be air dried prior to use.

18. The shelf life of glutaraldehyde if _____ days.
    A. 7-10   B. 10-14   C. 20-24   D. 24-28

19. In order to kill spores, an item must be immersed in a 2% aqueous solution of glutaraldehyde for _____ hours.
    A. 2   B. 6   C. 10   D. 12

20. _____ is a process in which air bubbles are imploded and burst inward causing the release of particles of soil or tissue debris.
    A. Sterilization
    B. Cavitation
    C. Autoclaving
    D. Decontamination

21. Which high level disinfectant is effective on surfaces, floors, and equipment?
    A. Sodium hypochlorite
    B. Alcohol
    C. Carbolic acid
    D. Quaternary ammonium compounds

22. Sodium hypochlorite forms a highly carcinogenic solution if it becomes mixed with
    A. alcohol
    B. betadine
    C. formaldehyde
    D. acetone

23. Which intermediate level disinfectant is a highly concentrated solution that can be easily diluted?
    A. Glutaraldehyde
    B. Sodium hypochlorite
    C. Alcohol
    D. Carbolic acid

24. Which intermediate level disinfectant is low cost, easy to mix with water, odorless, and non-corrosive on metals?
    A. Sodium hypochlorite
    B. Alcohol
    C. Carolic acid
    D. Quaternary ammonium compounds

25. Which intermediate level disinfectant is non-sporicidal, highly flammable, and effective against many microbes including HIV?
    A. Sodium hypochlorite
    B. Alcohol
    C. Carbolic acid
    D. Quaternary ammonium compounds

KEY (CORRECT ANSWERS)

1.	D	11.	A
2.	A	12.	C
3.	A	13.	C
4.	B	14.	D
5.	D	15.	B
6.	D	16.	A
7.	C	17.	A
8.	A	18.	D
9.	B	19.	C
10.	C	20.	B

21. A
22. C
23. D
24. D
25. D

TEST 2

DIRECTIONS: Each question or incomplete statement is followed by several suggested answers or completions. Select the one that BEST answers the question or completes the statement. *PRINT THE LETTER OF THE CORRECT ANSWER IN THE SPACE AT THE RIGHT.*

1. Which presoaking solution keeps organic debris moist? 1.____
   A. Enzymes
   B. Sterile water
   C. Alcohol
   D. Detergent

2. Which presoaking solution removes moistened and dried debris without the need for mechanical action? 2.____
   A. Enzymes
   B. Sterile water
   C. Alcohol
   D. Detergent

3. _____ is a surface acting agent that lowers the surface tension of a liquid so it can penetrate deeper and prevents debris from being re-deposited on the item to which the soil was attached. 3.____
   A. Lipase
   B. Amylase
   C. Surfactant
   D. Hydrogen peroxide

4. Bath temperatures over _____°F will coagulate protein and make it more difficult to remove. 4.____
   A. 80
   B. 100
   C. 120
   D. 140

5. What is the PROPER bath temperature for cleaning instruments? 5.____
   A. 70-99°F
   B. 80-109°F
   C. 90-119°F
   D. 100-129°F

6. _____ refers to the removal of any residue of cleaning agents and chemical remaining after the cleaning process and is necessary regardless of whether a manual or mechanical cleaning process was used. 6.____
   A. Impingement
   B. Free rinsing
   C. Decontaminating
   D. Disinfecting

7. _____ are chemicals that hold hard water minerals in solution and prevent soaps or detergents from reacting with the minerals. 7.____
   A. Protease enzymes
   B. Chelating agents
   C. Sequestering agents
   D. Detergents

8. _____ are chemicals that remove or inactive hard water minerals. 8.____
   A. Protease enzymes
   B. Chelating agents
   C. Sequestering agents
   D. Detergents

2 (#2)

9. Which type of wrapping is made of cotton or blends of cotton/polyester and must be inspected for lint, holes, worn areas, and stains?
    A. Woven textiles
    B. Woven textiles with barrier properties
    C. Non-woven materials
    D. Rigid instrument containers

9.____

10. Which type of wrapping is made of cotton/polyester blend, chemical treated for moisture resistances, and requires two wrappers per instrument set?
    A. Woven textiles
    B. Woven textiles with barrier properties
    C. Non-woven materials
    D. Rigid instrument containers

10.____

11. Which type of steam sterilizer tests for air removal daily with a Bowie-Dick test?
    A. Flash sterilization
    B. Autoclave
    C. Gravity displacement
    D. Pre-vacuum steam sterilizer

11.____

12. Which type of sterilization method uses radio frequency waves at a low temperature, is a dry process, sterilization occurs in one hour, and forms radicals that interact with the cell membrane which kills the microbes?
    A. Ozone gas sterilizer
    B. Chlorine dioxide gas
    C. Plasma sterilization
    D. Vapor phase hydrogen peroxide

12.____

13. Which type of sterilization oxidizes bacteria, is destructive to rubber and plastics, corrosive for some metals, and should not be used on long-cannulated instruments?
    A. Ozone gas sterilizer
    B. Chlorine dioxide gas
    C. Plasma sterilization
    D. Vapor phase hydrogen peroxide

13.____

14. The preparation and packaging must have an air exchange rate of _____ per hour.
    A. 4
    B. 6
    C. 8
    D. 10

14.____

15. What is the acceptable temperature range for the preparation and packaging area?
    A. 60-65°F
    B. 70-75°F
    C. 75-80°F
    D. 80-85°F

15.____

16. Which of the following represents the ideal humidity level in the preparation and packaging area?
    A. 20%
    B. 35%
    C. 40%
    D. 50%

16.____

17. Which of the following statements is TRUE when a non-perforated tray is used for the sterilization of instrument sets?
    A. Must be wrapped with a towel prior to instrument placement
    B. Must be processed on the top rack of the sterilizer
    C. Must be laid flat on the sterilizer rack
    D. Must be tilted on the sterilizer rack

17.____

18. Which of the following statements is TRUE regarding the floors of the preparation area?
    A. Should be wet-mopped daily
    B. Should be dry-mopped each shift
    C. Should be vacuumed once per week
    D. Should be broom-swept hourly

    18.____

19. When assembling an instrument set containing heavy and delicate objects, where should the heavier instruments be placed?
    A. On top of the delicate instruments
    B. On the bottom of the set
    C. In the center of the tray
    D. On the right-hand side

    19.____

20. Which of the following can be performed to assist in the drying of wrapped instrument sets?
    A. Place the set on a transfer tray.
    B. Place instruments in foam dividers.
    C. Place a towel in the bottom of the tray.
    D. Place silicone mats in the bottom of the tray.

    20.____

21. In what location should the chemical indicator be placed in a wrapped set of instruments?
    A. In the left-hand corner
    B. In the center of the set
    C. In two opposing corners
    D. On the right-hand side

    21.____

22. Where should chemical indicators be placed for multi-layer container systems?
    A. In the middle of the tray
    B. In the bottom level
    C. On each level
    D. In each corner

    22.____

23. What is the MAXIMUM size and weight of a textile pack?
    A. 10"x12"x12" / 20 lbs.
    B. 12"x20"x10" / 7.2 lbs.
    C. 12"x12"x12" / 10 lbs.
    D. 12"x12"x20" / 12 lbs.

    23.____

24. Which of the following statements is TRUE regarding preparation of basin sets for sterilization?
    A. Basins should be separated by at least ½ inch.
    B. Basins should be placed in opposing directions.
    C. An absorbent material should be placed between each basin.
    D. A non-absorbent material should be placed between each basin.

    24.____

25. All of the following are basic principles of packaging EXCEPT:
    A. A package must be able to be opened without contamination.
    B. Packing material must be acceptable for all types of sterilization.
    C. Packing material must allow the sterilant to reach the contents.
    D. The packing material must be a barrier to microorganisms.

    25.____

KEY (CORRECT ANSWERS)

1.	B	11.	D
2.	B	12.	C
3.	C	13.	A
4.	D	14.	A
5.	B	15.	B
6.	B	16.	C
7.	B	17.	D
8.	C	18.	A
9.	A	19.	D
10.	A	20.	C

21.	B
22.	C
23.	D
24.	C
25.	B

TEST 3

DIRECTIONS: Each question or incomplete statement is followed by several suggested answers or completions. Select the one that BEST answers the question or completes the statement. *PRINT THE LETTER OF THE CORRECT ANSWER IN THE SPACE AT THE RIGHT.*

1. Which of the following can inhibit the penetration of sterilant? 1.____
   A. A wrapper that is too small
   B. A wrapper that is too large
   C. An envelope fold on a small set
   D. A square fold on a large deck

2. Approximately how much space should be left between an item and the inside edges of a peel pouch? 2.____
   A. 1 inch   B. 2 inches   C. 3 inches   D. 4 inches

3. Which of the following packaging materials is acceptable for steam sterilization? 3.____
   A. Tyvek
   B. Polyethylene
   C. Aluminum foil
   D. Non-woven wraps

4. Which of the following packaging materials is acceptable for low-temperature glass plasma sterilization? 4.____
   A. Paper pouches
   B. Polyethylene
   C. Aluminum foil
   D. Non-woven wraps

5. Tamper-evident seals on rigid containers include 5.____
   A. lids and gaskets
   B. lids and latches
   C. latches and locks
   D. filters and gaskets

6. During the sterilization process, rigid containers must be placed 6.____
   A. flat
   B. on their side
   C. on the top shelf
   D. on the middle shelf

7. What series of stainless steel is used to manufacturer malleable retractors? 7.____
   A. 200   B. 300   C. 400   D. 500

8. Which of the following would be used to hold back the intestines during an abdominal procedure? 8.____
   A. Kelly clamp
   B. Deaver retractor
   C. Debakey forcep
   D. Greenberg retractor

9. What is the MOST difficult part of a hemostat to clean? 9.____
   A. Box lock   B. Ratchet   C. Shanks   D. Jaws

10. What is the FINAL stage in the process of manufacturing of a surgical grade instrument? 10.____
    A. Cavitation
    B. Lubrication
    C. Passivation
    D. Ebonization

11. Scissors with black handles are often referred to as
    A. satin
    B. martensitic
    C. super sharps
    D. surgical grade

12. The layer on a surgical instrument created by the passivation process is called
    A. satin finish
    B. tungsten carbide
    C. chromium oxide
    D. an ebonized surface

13. What is the EASIEST method to identify an instrument with tungsten carbide inserts?
    A. Black handles
    B. Gold handles
    C. Satin finish
    D. Shiny finish

14. What type of finish is on a surgical instrument that is used for laser procedures?
    A. Gold
    B. Satin
    C. Shiny
    D. Ebonized

15. Unless otherwise directed by the manufacturer, how often should an instrument be lubricated?
    A. After every use
    B. Daily
    C. Weekly
    D. Monthly

16. The air flow in the preparation and packaging area must be maintained at _____ pressure.
    A. positive
    B. negative
    C. constant
    D. automatic

17. For what time period should service records on sterilizer equipment be maintained?
    A. 1 year
    B. 3 years
    C. 5 years
    D. For the life of the equipment

18. A biological indicator is required with each sterilization cycle containing
    A. disposable items
    B. sharps
    C. heavy equipment
    D. implantable devices

19. How often do dynamic air removal sterilizers require the use of a Bowie-Dick test?
    A. After every load
    B. Daily
    C. Weekly
    D. Monthly

20. With what type of sterilization should the documentation be tracked directly to the patient for which the item was used?
    A. Flash sterilization
    B. Autoclave
    C. Gravity displacement
    D. Pre-vacuum steam sterilizer

21. If an employee has had an ethylene oxide exposure, records must be maintained _____ after employee's last day of employment.
    A. 30 days
    B. 6 months
    C. 10 years
    D. 30 years

22. Most manufacturers recommend testing high-level disinfectant solutions how often?
    A. Prior to each use
    B. Daily
    C. Weekly
    D. Monthly

23. Records are kept for facilities who treat newborn babies for a time period of _____ years.
    A. 7
    B. 10
    C. 18
    D. 21

24. Ethylene oxide sterilizers require more documentation than other types of low temperature sterilizers because ethylene oxide has been classified as a
    A. antigen
    B. pathogen
    C. carcinogen
    D. histogen

25. Which of the following must be affixed to each package that is sterilized to allow facility personnel to trace a sterilized package to the exact date and processing time, sterilizer, and load contents if there is a need for a recall?
    A. Biological indicator
    B. Chemical indicator
    C. Lot control number
    D. Load log

KEY (CORRECT ANSWERS)

1.	B	11.	C
2.	A	12.	C
3.	D	13.	B
4.	D	14.	D
5.	C	15.	A
6.	A	16.	A
7.	B	17.	D
8.	B	18.	D
9.	A	19.	B
10.	C	20.	A

21. D
22. A
23. D
24. C
25. C

TEST 4

DIRECTIONS: Each question or incomplete statement is followed by several suggested answers or completions. Select the one that BEST answers the question or completes the statement. *PRINT THE LETTER OF THE CORRECT ANSWER IN THE SPACE AT THE RIGHT.*

1. If an incident requires a report be sent to OSHA, the necessary paperwork must be submitted within a time period of _____ days.
   A. 8 B. 10 C. 14 D. 30

2. A work related death must be reported to OSHA within a time frame of _____ hours.
   A. 4 B. 8 C. 12 D. 24

3. All of the following agencies require that Central Service employees have been properly trained and competent in their job EXCEPT
   A. Joint Commission
   B. Centers of Medicare and Medicaid Services
   C. Occupational Safety and Health Administration
   D. Department of Environmental Protection

4. Which of the following parameters is NOT required to be documented for every run of a sterilizer cycle?
   A. Sterilizer temperature
   B. Room temperature
   C. Cycle time
   D. Name of Central Service Technician running the cycle

5. If you are asked to decontaminate an area that could possibly be contaminated with HIV, you should allow the area to be wet with disinfectant for a minimum time of _____ seconds.
   A. 30 B. 60 C. 120 D. 300

6. If you are asked to decontaminate an area that could possibly be contaminated with HIV, you should allow the area to be wet with disinfectant for a minimum time of _____ minute(s).
   A. 1 B. 3 C. 5 D. 10

7. As of January 1, 2015, which product is NOT permitted to be used in Central Service Departments?
   A. Ethylene oxide
   B. Hydrogen peroxide
   C. Oxyfume
   D. Ozone

8. If a product and its associated label contains an EPA registration number, this means that the product has been deemed
   A. hazardous
   B. a carcinogen
   C. safe for use
   D. not for humans

9. Which of the following is the MOST appropriate definition of the role of the Central Service Technician?
   A. To provide dependable service to enhance patient care
   B. To provide sterilization services on a rigid schedule
   C. To provide the delivery of supplies
   D. To provide direct patient care

10. Medical-grade kraft paper CANNOT be used with which type of sterilization process?
    A. Steam
    B. Ozone
    C. Ethylene oxide
    D. Low temperature gas plasma

11. During cycle counts, how are items that are infrequently used but have a high dollar amount classified?
    A. A
    B. B
    C. C
    D. D

12. Which of the following sets would be considered high risk for special prion processing?
    A. Abdominal
    B. Laparotomy
    C. Open heart
    D. Craniotomy

13. When dealing with rigid containers, which of the following testings defines the sterilizer's ability to perform under actual conditions?
    A. Biological
    B. Small load
    C. Chemical
    D. Maximum load

14. Which of the following statements is TRUE regarding capsules?
    A. Easier to eliminate than vegetative bacteria
    B. Harder to eliminate than spores
    C. Resistant to heat and chemicals
    D. Easily eliminated by antibiotics

15. Spongiform encephalopathy is caused by
    A. fungi
    B. prions
    C. viruses
    D. spores

16. If contamination has been removed from an item but further processing is still required, the item is said to be
    A. cleaned
    B. disinfected
    C. sterilized
    D. sanitized

17. Which of the following should occur PRIOR to cleaning and processing a medical device?
    A. Device should be examined for proper function.
    B. Obtain approval from biomedical engineer.
    C. Material compatibility testing must be performed.
    D. Manufacturer's instructions must be obtained.

18. For what reason do alkaline detergents work BEST for mechanical washers?
    A. Extended dry cycles
    B. Lack of friction during washing
    C. Can break down proteins
    D. Compatible with high water temperatures

3 (#4)

19. A(n) _____ detergent would be used to remove severe stains from stainless steel instruments.
    A. organic acid
    B. organic alkaline
    C. proteolytic enzyme
    D. lipolytic enzyme

19.____

20. Which of the following would be the BEST method for preventing biofilm formation on instruments?
    A. Use a metal bristled brush
    B. Use a chlorine-based cleaner
    C. Soak overnight in an enzyme solution
    D. Rinse with distilled water and dry

20.____

21. Which of the following would be the APPROPRIATE mechanical washer process to reduce the potential for corrosion?
    A. Alkaline wash, regular rinse, acid rinse
    B. Alkaline wash, acid rinse, regular rinse
    C. Regular rinse, alkaline wash, acid rinse
    D. Acid rinse, alkaline wash, regular rinse

21.____

22. What is the PROPER protocol for dealing with opened instruments that have not been used?
    Instruments should be
    A. repackaged and resterilized
    B. resterilized
    C. resterilized after the indictors have been changed
    D. completely reprocessed

22.____

23. What is the purpose of a tungsten carbide insert on a needle holder?
    A. To provide from friction than stainless steel
    B. To hold the suture needle better
    C. To grip smaller needles
    D. To allow for easier cleanliness inspections

23.____

24. What is the PROPER action if the temperature in the central service area is 70°F and the humidity is 69%?
    A. Humidity must be increased.
    B. Temperature must be lowered.
    C. All packages must be inspected for moisture.
    D. Continue with normal activities.

24.____

25. Which of the following statements is TRUE regarding individuals entering the preparation area?
    A. All individuals must sign in
    B. Must be an employee of the facility
    C. Must wear proper attire
    D. Must be at least 21 years of age

25.____

KEY (CORRECT ANSWERS)

1.	A	11.	A
2.	B	12.	D
3.	D	13.	D
4.	B	14.	C
5.	A	15.	B
6.	D	16.	A
7.	C	17.	D
8.	C	18.	B
9.	A	19.	A
10.	D	20.	D

21. B
22. D
23. B
24. D
25. C

TEST 5

DIRECTIONS: Each question or incomplete statement is followed by several suggested answers or completions. Select the one that BEST answers the question or completes the statement. *PRINT THE LETTER OF THE CORRECT ANSWER IN THE SPACE AT THE RIGHT.*

1. If a wrapper is to be used as a sterile field, how far over the table must it extend?
   A. 1 inch   B. 2 inches   C. 4 inches   D. 6 inches

   1.____

2. Rigid containers are considered to be a medical device and must have a 510k clearance from which agency?
   A. Environmental Protection Agency
   B. Food and Drug Administration
   C. Centers for Disease Control and Prevention
   D. World Health Organization

   2.____

3. Which of the following actions can eliminate the need for frequent instrument reprocessing?
   A. Establishing minimum stock quantities
   B. Using plastic bags for dust covers
   C. Ordering additional supplies
   D. Proper stock rotation

   3.____

4. Which of the following is the MOST important element involved with double peel pouching?
   A. The inner pouch must lay flat inside the outer pouch.
   B. The two pouches should be sealed together.
   C. The inner package must remain unsealed.
   D. The inner package should be folded to fit inside the outer pouch.

   4.____

5. Which of the following is the INITIAL step that should be taken with an instrument needs to be sterilized for immediate use?
   A. Instrument should be wrapped in a double thickness non-woven wrap.
   B. Biological indicator should be placed in the sterilizer.
   C. Instrument should be cleaned according to manufacturer's specifications.
   D. Instrument should be placed and sealed in a peel pouch.

   5.____

6. _____ will result if air has not been removed from a package within a steam sterilizer.
   A. Non-adherence of autoclave tape   B. Wet packs
   C. Drying of packaging material   D. Poor steam penetration

   6.____

7. Name the instrument in the illustration shown at the right.
   A. Rongeur
   B. Screwdriver
   C. Osteotome
   D. Scoville retractor

   7.____

8. Which of the following actions can be taken to avoid damage to medical/surgical supplies in the receiving area?
   A. Removing supplies from the original shipping cartons
   B. Avoiding temperature and humidity extremes
   C. Storing supplies at least 8 inches off the floor
   D. Storing supplies at least 18 inches off the ceiling

   8.____

9.

   The instrument in the above illustration is used for what purpose?
   A. Vascular procedures to avoid tissue damage
   B. Widen tracheal incisions
   C. Gouging out bone
   D. Scraping or debriding biological tissue

   9.____

10. Through what area is steam exhausted from the sterilizer?
    A. Chamber jacket   B. Chamber drain line
    C. Door gasket   D. Pressure gauge

    10.____

11. For what reason should textile packs be placed on their side during the sterilization process?
    A. To facilitate the drying process
    B. To facilitate air removal and steam penetration
    C. To allow for the maximum number of packs to be loaded
    D. For better response from chemical indicators

    11.____

12. What is the process employed by ethylene oxide to eliminate the presence of microorganisms?
    A. Cavitation   B. Oxidation
    C. Alkylation   D. Passivation

    12.____

13. Which of the following represents the normal concentration of hydrogen peroxide in a low temperature gas plasma sterilizer?
    A. 27%   B. 46%   C. 59%   D. 78%

14. Name the instrument in the illustration shown at the right.
    A. Weitlander Retractor
    B. Balfour Retractor
    C. Bookwalter Retractor
    D. Hibbs Retractor

15. Rigid sterilization containers should be biologically tested prior to
    A. purchasing
    B. testing the gaskets
    C. the placement of filters
    D. the first cycle of the day

16. Which of the following represents the optimum amount of a supply to order?
    A. Economical order quantity
    B. Perpetual inventory count
    C. Cycle count
    D. Reorder point

17. Which of the following terms is synonymous with par level inventory?
    A. Total exchange cart
    B. Demand distribution
    C. Just in time distribution
    D. Fixed inventory level

18. Which distribution system is designed to reduce storeroom inventory?
    A. Just in time
    B. Exchange carts
    C. Par level inventory
    D. Demand distribution

19. An exhaust hood over the ethylene oxide sterilizer is an example of a(n) _____ control.
    A. environmental
    B. emission
    C. biological
    D. engineering

20. If a chemical indicator responds to two or more critical parameters, it belongs to Class
    A. 2   B. 3   C. 4   D. 5

21. What is the PROPER method in which to place paper/plastic pouches in a sterilizer?
    A. Paper facing paper in a basket
    B. Plastic facing plastic in a basket
    C. Paper facing plastic in a basket
    D. On their edge between other packages

22. The instrument in the illustration shown at the right is used for what purpose?   22._____
    A. Severe scalp lacerations
    B. Clamp blood vessels
    C. Cut tissue
    D. Retract soft tissue

23. For what reason is it important to evenly distribute large instruments in a set?   23._____
    A. Make the set easier to carry
    B. Make the set easier to sort
    C. Make the set easier to dry
    D. Provide a more thorough sterilization

24. The MINIMUM length of time central service technicians should scrub their hands during washing is _____ seconds.   24._____
    A. 15   B. 30   C. 45   D. 60

25. Instrument marking tape should be wrapped around an instrument _____ times.   25._____
    A. 1-1.5   B. 2-2.5   C. 3-3.5   D. 4-4.5

KEY (CORRECT ANSWERS)

1.	D	11.	B
2.	B	12.	C
3.	D	13.	C
4.	A	14.	C
5.	C	15.	B
6.	D	16.	A
7.	C	17.	D
8.	A	18.	A
9.	A	19.	D
10.	B	20.	C

21. C
22. A
23. C
24. A
25. A

TEST 6

DIRECTIONS: Each question or incomplete statement is followed by several suggested answers or completions. Select the one that BEST answers the question or completes the statement. *PRINT THE LETTER OF THE CORRECT ANSWER IN THE SPACE AT THE RIGHT.*

1. Patients, visitors, and vendors are considered to be what kind of customers to the central service department? 1._____
   A. Internal customers
   B. External customers
   C. Exclusive customer
   D. Professional customers

2. Surgeons, emergency rooms, and endoscopy suites are considered to be what kind of customers to the central service department? 2._____
   A. Internal customers
   B. External customers
   C. Exclusive customer
   D. Professional customers

3. Which of the following would be considered a vendor concern? 3._____
   A. Employee education
   B. Employee efficiency
   C. Availability of product
   D. Quality of product

4. Which of the following would be considered a labor concern? 4._____
   A. Product repeatability
   B. Employee education
   C. Availability of product
   D. Quality of product

5. _____ is at the heart of any process to facilitate customer service. 5._____
   A. Common courtesy
   B. Mutual respect
   C. Shared vision
   D. Effective communication

6. Which of the five dimensions of service quality assessment includes the appearance of physical facilities, equipment, personnel, and communication materials? 6._____
   A. Tangibles
   B. Reliability
   C. Responsiveness
   D. Assurance

7. Which of the five dimensions of service quality assessment involves the knowledge and courtesy of employees and their ability to convey trust and confidence? 7._____
   A. Empathy
   B. Reliability
   C. Responsiveness
   D. Assurance

8. _____ are used to prevent the formation of blood clots. 8._____
   A. Sequential compression devices
   B. Continuous passive motion devices
   C. Patient controlled analgesia pumps
   D. Hypo/hyperemia machines

9. Which of the following is an example of a flexible endoscope?
   A. Cystoscope
   B. Bronchoscope
   C. Arthroscope
   D. Resectoscope

10. Which of the following statements is FALSE regarding labeling packages?
    A. For packs, labeling should be on the indicator tape not on the wrapper.
    B. For peel pouches, labeling should be on the plastic side of the pouch.
    C. Marking pen should contain nontoxic permanent ink.
    D. Label after sterilization to insure sterility.

11. _____ is defined as the number of microorganisms on a contaminated object.
    A. Biofilm
    B. Bioburden
    C. Biological indicator
    D. Biohazard

12. Which of the following is defined as the transport of heat from a location of higher temperature to an area of lower temperature by a flow or current of liquids or gases?
    A. Circulation
    B. Convection
    C. Transference
    D. Translocation

13. _____ is the process in which a substance produces a chemical reaction that causes a physical change in the material.
    A. Corrosion
    B. Convection
    C. Cavitation
    D. Passivation

14. A device entering sterile tissue is referred to as a _____ device.
    A. critical
    B. non-critical
    C. semi-critical
    D. hyper-critical

15. _____ is the process in which air is removed from water in an ultrasonic cleaner.
    A. Deionization
    B. Degassing
    C. Impingement
    D. Denaturing

16. Which of the following is a microorganism used to biologically monitor steam, low-temperature gas plasma, and paracetic acid sterilizers?
    A. Geobacillus stearothermophilus
    B. Clostridium difficile
    C. Methacillin-resistant Staphylococcus aureus
    D. Vancomycin-resistant enterococci

17. Which of the following is a high level disinfectant that can achieve high level disinfection in a 12-minute exposure time when used for manual immersion at room temperature, or in a 5-minute exposure time when used in an automated endoscope reprocessor?
    A. Glutaraldehyde
    B. Formaldehyde
    C. Ortho-phthaldehyde
    D. Paraldehyde

18. _____ is a process of heating fluid to a moderate temperature for a specific period of time to destroy bacteria without changing the chemical composition of the fluid.
    A. Passivation
    B. Oxidation
    C. Pasteurization
    D. Cavitation

    18._____

19. Steam that contains 3% entrained water is referred to as _____ steam.
    A. saturated
    B. distilled
    C. hydrolyzed
    D. entrenched

    19._____

20. A device that comes into contact with the mucous membranes is referred to as a _____ device.
    A. critical
    B. non-critical
    C. semi-critical
    D. hyper-critical

    20._____

21. The use of two separate layers of wrapping material to create a package within a package is referred to as _____ wrapping.
    A. serial
    B. simultaneous
    C. sequential
    D. standardized

    21._____

22. _____ steam is defined as water vapor in a state of equilibrium between condensation and evaporation.
    A. saturated
    B. distilled
    C. hydrolyzed
    D. superheated

    22._____

23. A table-top sterilizer has a chamber volume of no more than _____ cubic feet.
    A. 2
    B. 3
    C. 4
    D. 5

    23._____

24. The instrument shown above is used for what purpose?
    A. Vascular procedures to avoid tissue damage
    B. Widen tracheal incisions
    C. Gouging out bone
    D. Scraping or debriding biological tissue

    24._____

25. Which of the following is an inanimate object that serves as a transmission agent for microorganisms?
    A. Prion
    B. Fomite
    C. Aerobe
    D. Antigen

    25._____

KEY (CORRECT ANSWERS)

1.	B		11.	B
2.	A		12.	B
3.	C		13.	A
4.	B		14.	A
5.	D		15.	B
6.	A		16.	A
7.	D		17.	C
8.	A		18.	C
9.	B		19.	A
10.	D		20.	C

21. C
22. D
23. A
24. C
25. B

EXAMINATION SECTION
TEST 1

DIRECTIONS: Each question or incomplete statement is followed by several suggested answers or completions. Select the one that BEST answers the question or completes the statement. *PRINT THE LETTER OF THE CORRECT ANSWER IN THE SPACE AT THE RIGHT.*

1. Which of the following factors contributes MOST to infant mortality? 1____

    A. Motor vehicle accidents
    B. Congenital cardiac malformation
    C. Prematurity
    D. Acute renal failure
    E. Pneumonia

2. All of the following statements are true regarding tuberculosis in the United States EXCEPT: 2____

    A. Mortality and morbidity rates increase with age
    B. Mortality rates are higher for males than females
    C. The incidence is much higher among the poor than the rich
    D. In low incidence areas, such as the United States, most tuberculosis is exogenous
    E. In 2015, the reported incidence of clinical disease in the United States was 3.0/100,000 population

3. Tubercle bacilli CANNOT be destroyed by 3____

    A. heat
    B. cold
    C. ultraviolet light
    D. phenol
    E. tricresol solution

4. The MOST frequent reservoirs for tuberculosis disease are 4____

    A. badgers
    B. mosquitoes
    C. humans
    D. cats
    E. deer

5. The LEADING cause of death for people younger than age 65 in the United States is 5____

    A. heart disease
    B. cerebrovascular disease
    C. chronic obstructive pulmonary disease
    D. diabetes mellitus
    E. chronic liver disease

6. Cooling towers and air conditioning units serve as breeding grounds for 6____

    A. staphylococcus aureus
    B. klebsiella pneumoniae
    C. streptococcus pneumoniae
    D. L. pneumophilia
    E. histoplasma capsulatum

7. Diseases transmitted by mosquitoes, mites, and ticks can be prevented by all of the following precautions EXCEPT

   A. protective clothing
   B. mask and gloves
   C. insect repellents
   D. door and window screens
   E. more than one but not all of the above

8. The PRINCIPAL area of study in injury control is

   A. epidemiology
   B. prevention
   C. treatment
   D. rehabilitation
   E. all of the above

9. Benzene is MOST likely to be associated with _____ cancer.

   A. blood
   B. kidney
   C. liver
   D. brain
   E. bone

10. A _____ test is used when the patient's wishes can be inferred from his or her known religious, ethical, and/or lifestyle beliefs.

    A. subjective
    B. relative
    C. limited objective
    D. pure objective
    E. none of the above

11. It is NOT true that standard deviation

    A. is the positive square root of variance
    B. is the most useful measure of dispersion
    C. standardizes extreme values
    D. decreases when the sample size increases
    E. of a small size in a sample causes the sample mean to be close to each individual value

12. The difference between the highest and lowest values in a series is called the

    A. range
    B. variance
    C. standard deviation
    D. coefficient of variation
    E. none of the above

13. The ratio of the standard deviation of a series to the arithmetic mean of the series is known as the

    A. coefficient of variation
    B. range
    C. variance
    D. frequency
    E. prevalence

14. In a disease which is usually of acute onset, lasts a couple of weeks, and has a case fatality rate of 75 to 85%, the

    A. prevalence is always higher than that of annual incidence
    B. incidence is always higher than the prevalence
    C. prevalence and annual incidence are always equal
    D. mortality rate will be consistently high in all countries where the disease occurs
    E. none of the above

15. A random sample of 20,000 men is screened for a history of excessive sugar consumption and the presence of diabetes.
    This is called a _____ study.

    A. prospective
    B. historical
    C. cross-sectional population
    D. retrospective-prospective
    E. case control retrospective

16. Five hundred young adults who are known cocaine users are assembled together with a control group. Recognizable psychotics are excluded, and the remainder are followed for 3 years to see whether any psychoses develop in them.
    This is a _____ study.

    A. retrospective
    B. case control retrospective
    C. cross-sectional population
    D. cohort
    E. none of the above

17. The FIRST and most important thing for the epidemiologist to do during the investigation of a patient with a communicable disease is to investigate

    A. the first source of infection
    B. the mode of transmission
    C. how many people have been infected
    D. the accuracy of the diagnosis
    E. preventive control of the disease

18. The single MOST important measure for the prevention of typhoid fever in a community is

    A. a ceftriaxon prophylaxis for all persons who are exposed to the disease
    B. washing hands
    C. immunization of the high risk population
    D. hospitalization and treatment of all known carriers
    E. water purification

19. Diseases more likely to occur in women than in men include all of the following EXCEPT

    A. Raynaud's disease
    B. sarcoidosis
    C. gout
    D. systemic lupus erythematosus
    E. secondary hypothyroidism

20. Over the past 50 years, which of the following chronic conditions has experienced the greatest decline in mortality rate?

    A. Heart disease   B. Stroke
    C. Cancer   D. Pneumonia
    E. Influenza

21. The population having the HIGHEST frequency of thalassemia is the 21____

    A. Jews B. Italians C. Chinese
    D. Japanese E. Americans

22. Over the past ten years, the majority of individuals who were initially diagnosed with diabetes mellitus were in what age group? 22____

    A. 18-29 B. 30-39
    C. 50-59 D. 70-79
    E. 80-89

23. Of the following, the disease LARGELY confined to people born in temperate climate zones and manifested in early adult life is 23____

    A. diabetes B. multiple sclerosis
    C. thalassemia D. hypertension
    E. prostate cancer

24. Hepatitis A has the highest incidence rate in individuals in which age group? 24____

    A. 0-9 B. 10-19 C. 20-29
    D. 30-39 E. 50-59

25. Recurrent episodes of low grade fever and arthralgia FREQUENTLY affect workers in 25____

    A. slaughter houses B. cotton mills
    C. coal mines D. hospital laboratories
    E. none of the above

KEY (CORRECT ANSWERS)

1. C			11. C	
2. D			12. A	
3. B			13. A	
4. C			14. B	
5. A			15. C	
6. D			16. D	
7. B			17. D	
8. E			18. E	
9. A			19. C	
10. C			20. B	

21. B
22. C
23. B
24. C
25. A

TEST 2

DIRECTIONS: Each question or incomplete statement is followed by several suggested answers or completions. Select the one that BEST answers the question or completes the statement. *PRINT THE LETTER OF THE CORRECT ANSWER IN THE SPACE AT THE RIGHT.*

1. Risk factors for malignancies of the liver and intra-hepatic biliary tract may include all of the following EXCEPT

    A. alpha-1 antitrypsin deficiency
    B. aflatoxin
    C. gentamicin
    D. alcohol
    E. steroids

    1_____

2. The parasite associated with an increased risk for developing carcinoma of the biliary tree is

    A. ascaris lumbricoides B. balantidium coli
    C. cryptoporidium   D. colonorchis sinensis
    E. enterobias vermicular is

    2_____

3. Of the following, the immunization that should NOT be given to an individual who has received immune globulin within the previous 3 months is

    A. IPV   B. DTP   C. MMR
    D. HBIG E. none of the above

    3_____

4. Which of the following is the LEADING cause of maternal death among pregnancies with abortive outcomes?

    A. Rubella   B. Ectopic pregnancy
    C. Teratoma D. Defective germ cell
    E. Herpes simplex II

    4_____

5. All of the following are leading causes of maternal mortality in the United States EXCEPT

    A. anesthesia complication
    B. embolism
    C. hypertensive disease of pregnancy
    D. hemorrhage
    E. maternal age between 20 and 30

    5_____

6. _____ is NOT a reportable disease.

    A. Pulmonary tuberculosis   B. Mumps
    C. Measles   D. Choriomeningitis
    E. Meningococcal sepsis

    6_____

7. The scientific field dealing with the collection, classification, description, analysis, interpretation, and presentation of data is called

    A. distributions   B. statistics
    C. standard deviation   D. median
    E. cohort study

    7_____

73

8. What type of treatment regimen should be administered to an infant born to a mother with active gonorrhea?

   A. Single IM dose of ceftriaxone
   B. Single oral dose of azithromycin
   C. Dual therapy of ceftriaxone and azithromycin
   D. Dual therapy of ceftriaxone and spectinomycin
   E. None of the above

9. A precaution necessary for children in day care who have pneumococcal disease is _____ isolation.

   A. strict   B. contact   C. enteric
   D. respiratory   E. none of the above

10. Children who have ever had a life-threatening allergic reaction to _____ should not get the polio vaccine.

    A. gluten   B. peanuts   C. eggs
    D. antibiotics   E. pollen

11. Stillbirths or perinatal death is a result of _____ % of pregnancies in women with untreated early syphilis.

    A. 5   B. 10   C. 25   D. 40   E. 80

12. Strongyloidiasis is endemic in the tropics and subtropics, including the southern and southwestern United States. The single MOST important control measure is

    A. purification of water
    B. food cooked at a higher temperature
    C. sanitary disposal measure for human waste
    D. mass vaccination of exposed population
    E. detection and treatment of all infected persons

13. In a large population, the mode of transmission MOST difficult to prevent is _____ spread.

    A. vector   B. person to person
    C. airborne   D. droplet
    E. none of the above

14. Of the following, the factor contributing the MOST to infant mortality is

    A. seizures   B. prematurity   C. hypothyroidism
    D. congenital heart disease E. birth trauma

15. Point prevalence studies tend to have an over-representation of

    A. chronic cases   B. fatal cases   C. short-term cases
    D. healthy persons   E. all of the above

16. The PRIMARY function of the federal government in the Medicaid program is to

    A. set standards
    B. provide services in their own institutions *only*
    C. investigate *only* services rendered
    D. pay for services
    E. pay for nursing care *only*

Questions 17-21.

DIRECTIONS: In Questions 17 through 21, match the numbered description with the appropriate lettered term listed in Column I. Place the letter of the correct answer in the space at the right.

COLUMN I
A. Sensitivity
B. Specificity
C. Screening
D. Median
E. Mode

17. The MOST commonly occurring value in a series of values 17.____

18. The initial examination of an individual whose disease is not yet under medical care 18.____

19. May be calculated in an ongoing longevity study 19.____

20. The ability of a screening test to identify correctly those individuals who truly have the disease 20.____

21. The ability of a test to identify correctly those individuals who truly do not have the disease 21.____

Questions 22-25.

DIRECTIONS: In Questions 22 through 25, match the numbered definition with the appropriate lettered term listed in Column I. Place the letter of the correct answer in the space at the right.

COLUMN I
A. Efficiency
B. Validity
C. Reliability
D. Bias
E. Causality

22. The extent to which a test provides the same result on the same subject on two or more occasions 22.____

23. The extent to which the results of a test agree with the results of another test that is accepted as more accurate or closer to the truth 23.____

24. A systematic error that is unintentionally made 24.____

25. Denotes direct effect 25.____

KEY (CORRECT ANSWERS)

1.	C	11.	D
2.	D	12.	C
3.	C	13.	C
4.	B	14.	B
5.	E	15.	C
6.	D	16.	D
7.	B	17.	E
8.	C	18.	C
9.	E	19.	D
10.	D	20.	A

21. B
22. C
23. B
24. D
25. E

EXAMINATION SECTION
TEST 1

DIRECTIONS: Each question or incomplete statement is followed by several suggested answers or completions. Select the one that BEST answers the question or completes the statement. *PRINT THE LETTER OF THE CORRECT ANSWER IN THE SPACE AT THE RIGHT.*

Questions 1-4.

DIRECTIONS: Questions 1 through 4 are to be answered on the basis of the following information.

In a day care center of 30 children (20 females and 10 males), 7 boys develop hepatitis A over a 3-week period. During the next 8 weeks, an additional 2 boys and 5 girls develop the infection.

1. The attack rate of hepatitis A in this day care center is _____%.
   A. 20   B. 30   C. 40   D. 46.6   E. 54.5

2. The secondary attack rate of hepatitis A in this day care center is MOST NEARLY _____%.
   A. 20   B. 15   C. 23   D. 27   E. 10

3. The attack rate of hepatitis A for boys in this school is MOST NEARLY _____%.
   A. 16   B. 40   C. 50   D. 60   E. 64

4. The attack rate of hepatitis A for girls is MOST NEARLY _____%.
   A. 21   B. 24   C. 25   D. 27   E. 30

5. The epidemic curve suggests a common source outbreak with
   A. continuing common source outbreak
   B. fecal-oral transmission
   C. secondary airborne transmission
   D. secondary person-to-person transmission
   E. none of the above

6. The _____ rate is determined by the number of deaths caused by a specific disease divided by the number of cases of the disease.
   A. mortality   B. case fatality
   C. attack   D. cause specific death
   E. none of the above

7. Rate is the expression of the probability of occurrence of a particular event in a defined population during a specified period of time.
   The rate calculated for various segments of the population is known as the _____ rate.
   A. specific   B. crude
   C. adjusted   D. variable
   E. none of the above

8. The sources of disease surveillance data include all of the following EXCEPT

    A. individual case reports
    B. emergency room visit records
    C. hospital discharge summaries
    D. death certificates
    E. none of the above

9. All of the following are true about tularemia EXCEPT that it is

    A. a zoonotic disease
    B. more common during the summer months in the western states
    C. more common in winter months in the eastern states
    D. primarily transmitted by the bite of a spider
    E. none of the above

10. Which of the following is NOT among the basic steps in an investigation of an epidemic?

    A. Verification of diagnosis
    B. Establishing the existence of an epidemic
    C. Characterization of the distribution of cases
    D. Formulating a conclusion
    E. All of the above

11. The LAST step in conducting an epidemic investigation is to

    A. develop an hypothesis
    B. test the hypothesis
    C. formulate a conclusion
    D. institute control measures
    E. establish the diagnosis of an epidemic

12. The patients who are infected with an agent but never develop clinical symptoms of the disease are known as _____ carriers.

    A. incubatory   B. subclinical   C. chronic
    D. convalescent   E. clinical

13. All of the following are uses of epidemiology EXCEPT to

    A. identify factors that cause disease
    B. explain how and why diseases and epidemics occur
    C. establish a clinical diagnosis of disease
    D. determine a patient's prognosis
    E. evaluate the effectiveness of health programs

14. The biological traits that determine the occurrence of a disease include all of the following EXCEPT

    A. genetic characteristics   B. diet
    C. race   D. ethnic origin
    E. sex

15. The general factors of resistance in a human host include all of the following EXCEPT

   A. the immune system
   B. intact skin
   C. diarrhea
   D. normal bacterial flora
   E. gastric juices

16. All of the following are examples of direct contact transmission EXCEPT

   A. syphilis
   B. herpes
   C. hepatitis B
   D. sporotrichosis
   E. none of the above

17. The basic aims and specific goals of medical studies and clinical research do NOT include

   A. assessing health status or clinical characteristics
   B. eliminating all carriers of diseases
   C. determining and assessing treatment outcomes
   D. identifying and assessing risk factors
   E. all of the above

18. Incidence and prevalence studies usually concern all of the following EXCEPT

   A. the occurrence of disease
   B. a comparison of outcomes between different treatments
   C. adverse side effects of drugs
   D. the death rate for a certain disease
   E. none of the above

19. A case series report can address almost any clinical issue but it is MOST commonly used to describe

   A. clinical characteristics of a disease
   B. screening test results
   C. treatment outcomes
   D. an unexpected result or event
   E. none of the above

20. A comparison of chemotherapy to chemotherapy plus radiation for laryngeal carcinoma would be an appropriate topic for a(n)

   A. cohort study
   B. case control study
   C. clinical trial
   D. case series report
   E. incidence and prevalence study

21. The sum of all values in a series divided by the actual number of values in the series is known as the

   A. mode
   B. median
   C. geometric mean
   D. arithmetic mean
   E. none of the above

22. The MOST commonly occurring value in a series of values is the 22._____

    A. mode
    B. median
    C. geometric mean
    D. arithmetic mean
    E. none of the above

23. The ratio of the standard deviation of a series to the arithmetic mean of the series is known as the 23._____

    A. range
    B. variance
    C. coefficient of variation
    D. standard deviation
    E. epidemic curve

24. The sum of squared deviations from the mean divided by the number of values in the series minus 1 is called the 24._____

    A. range
    B. variance
    C. standard deviation
    D. coefficient of variation
    E. frequency polygon

25. The _____ is a tool for comparing categories of mutually exclusive discrete data. 25._____

    A. pie chart
    B. Venn diagram
    C. bar diagram
    D. histogram
    E. frequency polygon

KEY (CORRECT ANSWERS)

1.	D	11	D
2.	C	12.	B
3.	E	13.	D
4.	C	14.	B
5.	D	15.	A
6.	B	16.	E
7.	A	17.	B
8.	E	18.	B
9.	D	19.	A
10.	E	20.	C

21. D
22. A
23. C
24. B
25. C

TEST 2

DIRECTIONS: Each question or incomplete statement is followed by several suggested answers or completions. Select the one that BEST answers the question or completes the statement. *PRINT THE LETTER OF THE CORRECT ANSWER IN THE SPACE AT THE RIGHT.*

1. A _____ is a special form of the bar diagram used to represent categories of continuous and ordered data.

    A. pie chart
    B. histogram
    C. Venn diagram
    D. cumulative frequency graph
    E. frequency polygon

    1.____

2. A medical student performs venipuncture on 1,000 randomly selected patients and is successful on the first attempt 700 times.
What is the probability that her next venipuncture will be successful on the first attempt?

    A. 7%   B. 14%   C. 50%   D. 70%   E. 80%

    2.____

3. All of the following are true regarding the standard error of the mean of a sample EXCEPT that it

    A. is an estimate of the standard deviation of the population
    B. is based on a normal distribution
    C. increases as the sample size increases
    D. is used to determine confidence limits
    E. none of the above

    3.____

4. All of the following are characteristics of a confidence interval EXCEPT that it

    A. is based on a critical ratio when the sample is large
    B. gives an indication of the likely magnitude of the true value
    C. gives an indication of the certainty of the point estimate
    D. becomes narrower as the sample size increases
    E. none of the above

    4.____

5. Nonparametric tests can be used to compare two populations with which of the following conditions?

    A. Each population is unimodal
    B. Both populations have equal numbers
    C. Each population is independent
    D. Each population is distributed normally
    E. All of the above

    5.____

6. All of the following vaccines are grown in embryonated chicken eggs EXCEPT

    A. yellow fever   B. measles   C. mumps
    D. rubella   E. influenza

    6.____

7. Which of the following vaccines should NOT be given to individuals who live in households with an immuno-compromised host?

   A. Yellow fever
   B. Hepatitis B
   C. Oral polio
   D. Influenza
   E. Diphtheriae

8. A solution of antibodies derived from the serum of animals immunized with a specific antigen is a(n)

   A. immunoglobulin
   B. antitoxin
   C. toxoid
   D. vaccine
   E. none of the above

9. All of the following may be significant sequale of measles infection EXCEPT

   A. pneumonia
   B. encephalitis
   C. congenital birth defects
   D. mental retardation
   E. death

10. All of the following statements about vaccination during pregnancy are true EXCEPT:

    A. Live attenuated viral vaccines should not be given to pregnant women
    B. Pregnant women at substantial risk of exposure may receive a live viral vaccine
    C. There is evidence that inactivated vaccines also pose risks to the fetus
    D. There is no evidence that immunoglobulins pose any risk to the fetus
    E. None of the above

11. None of the following conditions are reasons for delaying or discontinuing routine immunizations EXCEPT

    A. soreness, redness or swelling at the injection site in reaction to previous immunization
    B. a temperature of more than 105F in reaction to previous DTP vaccine
    C. mild diarrheal illness in an otherwise well child
    D. current antimicrobial therapy
    E. breastfeeding

12. Children and infants with any of the following disorders should not receive pertussis vaccine EXCEPT those with

    A. uncontrolled epilepsy
    B. infantile spasms
    C. progressive encephalopathy
    D. developmental delay
    E. none of the above

13. Which of the following groups of patients should NOT receive pneumococcal polysaccharide vaccine?

    A. Elderly, age 65 or older
    B. Immunocompromised
    C. Children age 2 years or older with anatomic or functional asplenia

D. Children age 2 years or older with nephrotic syndrome or CSF leaks
E. Children under 2 years of age

14. All of the following are significant complications of sexually transmitted diseases in women EXCEPT

    A. pelvic inflammatory disease
    B. infertility
    C. teratogenicity
    D. cancer
    E. ectopic pregnancy

14.____

15. For primary prevention and maximal safety, a person should

    A. engage in a mutually monogamous relationship
    B. limit the number of sexual partners
    C. inspect and question new partners
    D. avoid sexual practices involving anal or fecal contact
    E. all of the above

15.____

16. All of the following are complications caused by untreated syphilis infection EXCEPT

    A. obesity
    B. blindness
    C. psychosis
    D. cardiovascular disease
    E. none of the above

16.____

17. All of the following statements are true regarding syphilis EXCEPT:

    A. The organism cannot enter through intact skin
    B. Everyone is susceptible
    C. There is no natural or acquired immunity
    D. No vaccine is available
    E. Reinfection is rare

17.____

18. Which of the following sexually transmitted diseases rank as the number one reported communicable disease in the United States?

    A. Syphilis
    B. Gonorrhea
    C. AIDS
    D. Chlamydia
    E. Hepatitis B

18.____

19. Which of the following is believed to be the MOST common sexually transmitted bacterial pathogen in the United States?

    A. Treponema pallidum
    B. Chlamydia trachomatis
    C. Nisseriae gonorrhea
    D. E. coli
    E. Herpes zoster

19.____

20. All of the following are documented modes of transmission for human immunodeficiency virus EXCEPT _____ transmission.

    A. sexual
    B. percutaneous exposure
    C. airborne
    D. mother to child
    E. none of the above

20.____

21. In order to prevent HIV infection, which of the following groups should NOT donate blood?

    A. Any man who has had sexual contact with another man since 1977
    B. Present or past IV drug abusers
    C. Individuals from Central Africa and Haiti
    D. Sexual partners of any of the above groups
    E. All of the above

22. Chlamydia trachomatis, the causative agent of chlamydia infection, has all of the following characteristics EXCEPT it

    A. grows only intracellularly
    B. contains both DNA and RNA
    C. is a protozoa
    D. divides by binary fission
    E. has cell walls similar to gram-negative bacteriae

23. All of the following are true regarding the resultant effects of chlamydia trachomatis EXCEPT:

    A. Approximately 50% cases of non-gonococcal urethritis in men
    B. 99% of cases of pelvic inflammatory disease
    C. Mucopurulent cervicitis
    D. Inclusion conjunctivitis in infants born to infected mothers
    E. Acute epididymitis in men

24. All of the following statements are true regarding hepatitis A infection EXCEPT:

    A. Approximately 70% of Americans are infected by the age of 20
    B. Incidence appears to be declining
    C. Infection is related to age and socioeconomic status
    D. The incubation period is 15-50 days with an average of 28-30 days
    E. Young children are more likely to have subclinical infections

25. The transmission of hepatitis A virus is facilitated by all of the following EXCEPT

    A. poor personal hygiene
    B. poor sanitation
    C. drinking out of the same cup
    D. eating uncooked or raw food
    E. eating food contaminated by human hands after cooking

KEY (CORRECT ANSWERS)

1. B
2. D
3. C
4. E
5. E

6. D
7. C
8. B
9. C
10. C

11. B
12. D
13. E
14. C
15. E

16. A
17. E
18. B
19. B
20. C

21. E
22. C
23. B
24. A
25. C

EXAMINATION SECTION
TEST 1

DIRECTIONS: Each question or incomplete statement is followed by several suggested answers or completions. Select the one that BEST answers the question or completes the statement. *PRINT THE LETTER OF THE CORRECT ANSWER IN THE SPACE AT THE RIGHT.*

1. The MOST common cause of death before age 65 is   1.____
   - A. cerebrovascular disease
   - B. malignant neoplasm
   - C. heart disease
   - D. diabetes mellitus
   - E. liver cirrhosis

2. Of the following, the disease NOT transmitted by mosquitoes is   2.____
   - A. dengue fever
   - B. lymphocytic choriomeningitis
   - C. western equine encephalitis
   - D. St. Louis encephalitis
   - E. yellow fever

3. The single MOST effective measure to prevent hookworm infection is   3.____
   - A. washing hands
   - B. washing clothes daily
   - C. cooking food at high temperatures
   - D. wearing shoes
   - E. none of the above

4. Transmission of tuberculosis in the United States occurs MOST often by   4.____
   - A. fomites
   - B. blood transfusion
   - C. inhalation of droplet
   - D. transplacentally
   - E. milk

5. The second MOST common cause of death in the United States is   5.____
   - A. accident
   - B. cancer
   - C. cerebrovascular disease
   - D. heart disease
   - E. AIDS

6. All of the following bacteria are spread through fecal-oral transmission EXCEPT   6.____
   - A. haemophilus influenza type B
   - B. campylobacter
   - C. escherichia coli
   - D. salmonella
   - E. shigella

7. Routine immunization is particularly important for children in day care because pre-school-aged children currently have the highest age specific incidence of all of the following EXCEPT   7.____
   - A. H-influenzae type B
   - B. neisseria meningitis
   - C. measles
   - D. rubella
   - E. pertussis

8. Hand washing and masks are necessary for physical contact with all of the following patients EXCEPT

   A. lassa fever
   B. diphtheria
   C. coxsackie virus disease
   D. varicella
   E. plaque

9. Control measures for prevention of tick-borne infections include all of the following EXCEPT:

   A. Tick-infested area should be avoided whenever possible.
   B. If a tick-infested area is entered, protective clothing that covers the arms, legs, and other exposed area should be worn.
   C. Tick/insect repellent should be applied to the skin.
   D. Ticks should be removed promptly.
   E. Daily inspection of pets and removal of ticks is not indicated.

10. The PRINCIPAL reservoir of giardia lamblia infection is

    A. humans
    B. mosquitoes
    C. rodents
    D. sandflies
    E. cats

11. Most community-wide epidemics of giardia lamblia infection result from

    A. inhalation of droplets
    B. eating infected meats
    C. eating contaminated eggs
    D. drinking contaminated water
    E. blood transfusions

12. Epidemics of giardia lamblia occurring in day care centers are USUALLY caused by

    A. inhalation of droplets
    B. person-to-person contact
    C. fecal and oral contact
    D. eating contaminated food
    E. all of the above

13. Measures of the proportion of the population exhibiting a phenomenon at a particular time is called the

    A. incidence
    B. prevalence
    C. prospective study
    D. cohort study
    E. all of the above

14. The occurrence of an event or characteristic over a period of time is called

    A. incidence
    B. prevalence
    C. specificity
    D. case control study
    E. cohort study

15. All of the following are live attenuated viral vaccines EXCEPT

    A. measles
    B. mumps
    C. rubella
    D. rabies
    E. yellow fever

16. Chlorinating air-cooling towers can prevent

    A. scarlet fever
    B. impetigo
    C. typhoid fever
    D. mycobacterium tuberculosis
    E. legionnaire's disease

17. Eliminating the disease causing agent may be done by all of the following methods EXCEPT

    A. chemotherapeutic
    B. cooling
    C. heating
    D. chlorinating
    E. disinfecting

18. Which of the following medications is used to eliminate pharyngeal carriage of neisseria meningitidis?

    A. Penicillin
    B. Rifampin
    C. Isoniazid
    D. Erythromycin
    E. Gentamicin

19. Post-exposure prophylaxis is recommended for rabies after the bite of all of the following animals EXCEPT

    A. chipmunks
    B. skunks
    C. raccoons
    D. bats
    E. foxes

20. To destroy the spores of clostridium botulinum, canning requires a temperature of AT LEAST _____ °C.

    A. 40
    B. 60
    C. 80
    D. 100
    E. 120

21. All of the following are killed or fractionated vaccines EXCEPT

    A. hepatitis B
    B. yellow fever
    C. H-influenza type B
    D. pneumococcus
    E. rabies

22. Of the following, the disease NOT spreadly by food is

    A. typhoid fever
    B. shigellosis
    C. typhus
    D. cholera
    E. legionellosis

23. In the United States, the HIGHEST attack rate of sheigella infection occurs in children between _____ of age.

    A. 1 to 6 months
    B. 6 months to 1 year
    C. 1 to 4 years
    D. 6 to 10 years
    E. 10 to 15 years

24. Risk factors for cholera include all of the following EXCEPT

    A. occupational exposure
    B. lower socioeconomic
    C. unsanitary condition
    D. high socioeconomic
    E. high population density in low income areas

25. The MOST common cause of traveler's diarrhea is 25.___
    A. escherichia coli
    B. shigella
    C. salmonella
    D. cholera
    E. campalobacter

KEY (CORRECT ANSWERS)

1.	C	11.	D
2.	B	12.	B
3.	D	13.	B
4.	C	14.	A
5.	B	15.	D
6.	A	16.	E
7.	B	17.	B
8.	C	18.	B
9.	E	19.	A
10.	A	20.	E

21. B
22. C
23. C
24. D
25. A

TEST 2

DIRECTIONS: Each question or incomplete statement is followed by several suggested answers or completions. Select the one that BEST answers the question or completes the statement. *PRINT THE LETTER OF THE CORRECT ANSWER IN THE SPACE AT THE RIGHT.*

1. The increased prevalence of entamoeba histolytica infection results from

    A. lower socioeconomic status in endemic area
    B. institutionalized (especially mentally retarded) population
    C. immigrants from endemic area
    D. promiscuous homosexual men
    E. all of the above

2. The MOST common infection acquired in the hospital is _____ infection.

    A. surgical wound
    B. lower respiratory tract
    C. urinary tract
    D. bloodstream
    E. gastrointestinal

3. The etiologic agent of Rocky Mountain spotted fever is

    A. rickettsia prowazekii
    B. rickettsia rickettsii
    C. rickettsia akari
    D. coxiella burnetii
    E. rochalimaena quintana

4. The annual death rate for injuries per 100,000 in both sexes is HIGHEST in those _____ years of age.

    A. 1 to 10
    B. 10 to 20
    C. 30 to 40
    D. 50 to 60
    E. 80 to 90

5. The death rate per 100,000 population due to motor vehicle accident is HIGHEST among

    A. whites
    B. blacks
    C. Asians
    D. native Americans
    E. Spanish surnamed

6. Among the following, the HIGHEST rate of homicide occurs in

    A. whites
    B. blacks
    C. native Americans
    D. Asians
    E. Spanish surnamed

7. All of the following are true statements regarding coronary heart disease EXCEPT:

    A. About 4.6 million Americans have coronary heart disease.
    B. Men have a greater risk of MI and sudden death.
    C. Women have a greater risk of angina pectoris.
    D. 25% of coronary heart disease death occurs in individuals under the age of 65 years.
    E. White women have a greater risk of MI and sudden death.

8. Major risk factors for coronary heart disease include all of the following EXCEPT

    A. smoking
    B. elevated blood pressure
    C. obesity
    D. high level of serum cholesterol
    E. family history of coronary heart disease

9. The MOST common cancer in American men is

    A. stomach   B. lung   C. leukemia
    D. prostate   E. skin

10. The HIGHEST incidence of prostate cancer occurs in _____ Americans.

    A. white   B. black   C. Chinese
    D. Asian   E. Spanish

11. All of the following are risk factors for cervical cancer EXCEPT

    A. smoking
    B. low socioeconomic condition
    C. first coital experience after age 20
    D. multiple sexual partners
    E. contracting a sexually transmitted disease

12. All of the following are independent adverse prognostic factors for lung cancer EXCEPT

    A. female sex
    B. short duration of symptom
    C. small cell histology
    D. metastatic disease at time of diagnosis
    E. persistently elevated CEA

13. Assuming vaccines with 80% efficacy were available in limited quantity, which vaccine among the following should be given to a military recruit?

    A. Polio   B. Pseudomonas
    C. Meningococcus   D. Influenza
    E. None of the above

14. Among the following, the vaccine which should be administered to children with sickle cell disease is

    A. influenza   B. meningococcus
    C. pseudomonas   D. pneumococcal
    E. yellow fever

15. All of the following are correct statements concerning gastric carcinoma in the United States EXCEPT:

    A. The risk for males is 2.2 times greater than for females.
    B. The incidence is increased.
    C. The risk is higher in persons with pernicious anemia than for the general population.

D. City dwellers have an increased risk of stomach cancer.
E. Workers with high levels of exposure to nickle and rubber are at increased risk.

16. During the first year of life, a condition that can be detected by screening is

    A. hypothyroidism
    B. RH incompatibility
    C. phenylketonuria
    D. congenital dislocation of the hip
    E. all of the above

17. The major reservoir of the spread of tuberculosis within a hospital is through

    A. patients   B. custodial staff
    C. doctors   D. nursing staff
    E. undiagnosed cases

18. All of the following statements are true regarding tuberculosis EXCEPT:

    A. Droplet nuclei are the major vehicle for the spread of tuberculosis infection.
    B. The highest incidence is among white Americans.
    C. There is a higher incidence of tuberculosis in prison than in the general population.
    D. HIV infection is a significant independent risk factor for the development of tuberculosis.
    E. A single tubercle bacillus, once having gained access to the terminal air spaces, could establish infection.

19. The human papiloma virus is associated with

    A. kaposi sarcoma
    B. hepatoma
    C. cervical neoplasia
    D. nasopharyngeal carcinoma
    E. none of the above

20. General recommendations for prevention of sexually transmitted diseases include all of the following EXCEPT

    A. contact tracing   B. disease reporting
    C. barrier methods   D. prophylactic antibiotic use
    E. patient education

21. Syphilis remains an important sexually transmitted disease because of all of the following EXCEPT its

    A. public health heritage
    B. effect on perinatal morbidity and mortality
    C. association with HIV transmission
    D. escalating rate among black teenagers
    E. inability to be prevented

22. Which of the following statements about homicide is NOT true? Approximately

    A. forty percent are committed by friends and acquaintances
    B. twenty percent is committed by spouse
    C. fifteen percent is committed by a member of the victim's family
    D. fifteen percent is committed by strangers
    E. fifteen percent are labeled *relationship unknown*

23. Conditions for which screening has proven cost-effective include

    A. phenylketonuria
    B. iron deficiency anemia
    C. lead poisoning
    D. tuberculosis
    E. all of the above

24. Suicide is MOST common among

    A. whites
    B. blacks
    C. hispanics
    D. Asians
    E. none of the above

25. The MOST frequenty used method of suicide is

    A. hanging
    B. poisoning by gases
    C. firearms
    D. drug overdose
    E. drowning

KEY (CORRECT ANSWERS)

1. E
2. C
3. B
4. E
5. D
6. B
7. E
8. C
9. D
10. B
11. C
12. A
13. C
14. D
15. B
16. E
17. E
18. B
19. C
20. D
21. E
22. B
23. E
24. A
25. C

MICROBIOLOGY / PATHOLOGY

EXAMINATION SECTION
TEST 1

DIRECTIONS: Each question or incomplete statement is followed by several suggested answers or completions. Select the one that BEST answers the question or completes the statement. PRINT THE LETTER OF THE CORRECT ANSWER IN THE SPACE AT THE RIGHT.

1. True bacteria multiply by

    A. budding
    B. sexual fusion
    C. binary fission
    D. fragmentation of mycelia
    E. formation of sexual spores

2. Primary infection with coccidioidomycosis generally affects the

    A. liver
    B. spleen
    C. brain
    D. lungs
    E. lymph nodes

3. The antiviral action of interferon is due to

    A. interference with replication of virus
    B. interference with adsorption of virus to cells
    C. production of antibody against theinvading virus
    D. prevention of viral penetration
    E. destruction of antibody against the invading virus

4. The MOST conspicuous clinical sign of right-sided heart failure is

    A. hypertension
    B. mitral stenosis
    C. pulmonary edema
    D. systemic venous congestion
    E. brown induration of the lung

5. The capacity to grow in either filamentous or yeast form is termed

    A. dimorphism
    B. eumorphism
    C. parthenogenesis
    D. hermaphroditism
    E. allomorphism

6. In antibody synthesis, the *predominant* cell-type is the

    A. mast cell
    B. giant cell
    C. lymphocyte
    D. macrophage
    E. plasma cell

7. With respect to its histologic appearance, biologic behavior, and pre-invasive states, oral cancer MOST closely resembles the *most common* form of

    A. carcinoma of the colon
    B. carcinoma of the lung
    C. Hodgkin's disease
    D. cervical cancer
    E. breast cancer

8. Hypothyroidism in children results in

    A. myxedema   B. gigantism   C. cretinism
    D. acromegaly   E. diabetes insipidus

9. A transudate differs from an exudate in that the transudate has

    A. a cloudy appearance
    B. a higher specific gravity
    C. a lower protein concentration
    D. numerous erythrocytes
    E. a characteristic cellular component

10. In hematology, a "shift to the left" infers an increase in circulating

    A. monocytes   B. erythrocytes
    C. thromboeytes   D. immature neutrophils
    E. segmented neutrophils

11. Interstitial pulmonary inflammation is MOST characteristic of

    A. lobar pneumonia   B. viral pneumonia
    C. bronchial asthma   D. bronchopneumonia
    E. streptococcal pneumonia

12. Granulation tissue usually contains all of the following EXCEPT

    A. lymphocytes   B. fibroblasts   C. giant cells
    D. macrophages   E. capillary buds

13. Osteoporosis may be associated with each of the following EXCEPT

    A. prolonged corticosteroid administration
    B. prolonged immobilization
    C. chronic malnutrition
    D. hypervitaminosis D
    E. advanced ag

14. Jaundice is usually a result of each of the following EXCEPT

    A. gallstones   B. hemolytic anemia
    C. infectious hepatitis   D. vitamin K deficiency
    E. carcinomatous involvement of the common bile duct

15. The form of bacterial gene transfer which is *least* susceptible to DNAase and does NOT require cell-to-cell contact is

    A. transition   B. conjugation   C. transduction
    D. transformation   E. induction

16. The predominant bacteria found in saliva are

    A. vibrios   B. spirochetes   C. lactobacilli
    D. streptococci   E. fusiform bacilli

17. The mechanism of fibrin formation in damaged tissue is initiated by the

    A. release of thromboplastin from damaged cells
    B. release of calcium from damaged cells
    C. formation of thrombin from the interaction of prothrombin and fibrinogen
    D. interaction of thrombin and calcium
    E. release of lymphocytes from undamaged cells

18. A neoplasm composed of either blood vessels or lymph vessels is designated as

    A. angioma   B. hematoma   C. papilloma
    D. blue nevus   E. lymphosarcoma

19. An endocrine disease characterized by increased susceptibility to infection, increased fatigability, recessive inheritance, and polyuria is

    A. acromegaly   B. Graves' disease
    C. diabetes mellitus   D. Cushing's disease
    E. Hashimoto's disease

20. Rickettsial diseases can be diagnosed in the laboratory using certain strains of *Proteus vulgaris* because the rickettsia and these bacteria

    A. are morphologically similar
    B. have certain antigens in common
    C. produce similar pathogenic changes
    D. have similar physiologic characteristics
    E. are morphologically different

21. When a thrombotic embolus originates in a femoral vein, it usually becomes arrested in the

    A. right heart   B. renal circulation
    C. portal circulation   D. hepatic circulation
    E. pulmonary circulation

22. Which of the following malignancies has the *BEST* prognosis?

    A. Osteosarcoma   B. Multiple myeloma
    C. Basal cell carcinoma   D. Carcinoma of the breast
    E. Carcinoma of the esophagus

23. Which of the following neoplasms is *PRIMARY* in the adrenal medulla?

    A. Pheoehromocytoma   B. Arrhenoblastema
    C. Eosinophilic adenoma   D. Hürthle cell tumor
    E. None of the above

24. In *which* of the following bacterial infections is there a lysogenic virus that may be responsible for toxin production?

    A. Syphilis   B. Gonorrhea   C. Diphtheria
    D. Candidiasis   E. None of the above

25. Which of the following is formed in large quantities during the degradation of glucose by homofermentative *Streptococcus mutans*?

    A. Marinitol
    B. Lactic acid
    C. Acetic acid
    D. Butyric acid
    E. Propionic acid

25. ___

KEY (CORRECT ANSWERS)

1.	C	11.	B
2.	D	12.	C
3.	A	13.	D
4.	D	14.	D
5.	A	15.	C
6.	E	16.	D
7.	D	17.	A
8.	C	18.	A
9.	C	19.	C
10.	D	20.	B

21. E
22. C
23. A
24. C
25. B

TEST 2

DIRECTIONS: Each question or incomplete statement is followed by several suggested answers or completions. Select the one that BEST answers the question or completes the statement. PRINT THE LETTER OF THE CORRECT ANSWER IN THE SPACE AT THE RIGHT.

1. Bacterial spores are a problem in sterilizing instruments and equipment because 1.____

   A. they are resistant to antibiotics
   B. they are easy to kill, but are usually protected by organic matter
   C. they are resistant to physical and chemical agents
   D. most pathogenic bacteria are spore-formers
   E. few pathogenic bacteria are spore-formers

2. Koplik's spots on the buccal mucosa are pathognomonic for 2.____

   A. rubella B. rubeola C. roseola
   D. varicella E. Coxsackie virus A

3. Splenic infarcts MOST commonly result from emboli from the 3.____

   A. lungs B. deep leg veins
   C. left side of the heart D. right side of the heart
   E. left side of the brain

4. A 59-year-old male who demonstrates urinary retention or difficulty in voiding his bladder *most likely* has 4.____

   A. carcinoma of the prostate
   B. malignant neoplasm of the ureter
   C. benign prostatic hyperplasia (hypertrophy)
   D. bladder metastasis of bronchogenic carcinoma
   E. carcinoma of the colon

5. The change of a more specialized cell-type to a less specialized cell-type is 5.____

   A. dysplasia B. neoplasia C. metaplasia
   D. hyperplasia E. hypoplasia

6. Osteoporosis, metastatic calcification, renal stones, giant cell granulomas, and increased serum calcium levels are manifestations of 6.____

   A. hypothyroidism B. hyperthyroidism
   C. hyperadrenalism D. hypoparathyroidism
   E. hyperparathyroidism

7. An afebrile adult relates a 4-month history of chronic subcutaneous swelling over the angle of the mandible associated with intermittent, purulent drainage. Clinically, sinus tracts and scarring are present.
   In the differential diagnosis, one should consider 7.____

   A. tuberculosis B. herpes zoster
   C. actinomycosis D. histoplasmosis
   E. tertiary syphilis

8. An oral disease characterized by white patches on the buccal mucous membranes which consist largely of pseudo-mycelium and with minimal erosion of the membranes, is caused by

    A. Candida albicans
    B. Treponema pallidum
    C. Entamoeba histolytica
    D. Sporothrichum schenckii
    E. Corynebacterium diphtheriae

9. The MOST predominant organisms found in dental plaque are

    A. diplococci
    B. streptococci
    C. lactobacilli
    D. staphylococci
    E. eorynebacteria

10. Red (hemorrhagic) infarcts are MOST frequently found in the

    A. lung   B. brain   C. spleen   D. kidney   E. colon

11. The pathogenesis of jaundice in patients with infectious hepatitis is the result of

    A. massive hemolysis
    B. damage to liver cells
    C. massive fibrosis of liver
    D. obstruction of biliary tree
    E. portal hypertension

12. The etiologic agent of rubella is

    A. group B streptococcus
    B. Coxsackie virus
    C. adenovirus
    D. myxovirus
    E. poxvirus

13. The chemical constituents of bacteria and viruses which are MOST sensitive to ultraviolet irradiation are

    A. lipids
    B. proteins
    C. carbohydrates
    D. nucleic acids
    E. inorganic salts

14. Chronic passive congestion of the lungs is MOST often secondary to

    A. malnutrition
    B. massive hemorrhage
    C. cor pulmonale
    D. atherosclerotic heart disease
    E. obesity

15. A benign glandular neoplasm is termed

    A. cyst   B. nevus   C. adenoma   D. papilloma   E. ozena

16. The *initial* lesion of syphilis is a

    A. bubo
    B. gumma
    C. chancre
    D. pustule
    E. mucous patch

17. Prolonged anti-bacterial antibiotic therapy may predispose to infectious disease caused by the indigenous oral microorganism,

    A. *Fusobacterium fusiforme*
    B. *Streptococcus mitis*
    C. *Treponema microdentium*
    D. *Actinomyces israelii*
    E. *Candida albicans*

18. Generally, the antibiotic of choice for prophylactic therapy covering dental procedures in the patient with a heart valve abnormality is

    A. penicillin
    B. lincomycin
    C. tetracycline
    D. streptomycin
    E. erythromycin

19. Enzymes responsible for suppuration are derived CHIEFLY from

    A. serum
    B. tissue
    C. neutrophils
    D. lymphocytes
    E. plasma cells

20. Ethylene oxide is an agent that

    A. reversibly inhibits growth
    B. is antiseptic
    C. disinfects
    D. sterilizes
    E. cleanses

21. Which genus is *most likely* involved in bacillary dysentery?

    A. *Vibrio*
    B. *Proteus*
    C. *Shigella*
    D. *Entamoeba*
    E. *Salmonella*

22. Which of the following is a form of histiocytosis X?

    A. Porphyria
    B. Acromegaly
    C. Niemann-Pick disease
    D. Osteitis fibrosa cystica
    E. Hand-Schuller-Christian disease

23. The requirement for an insect vector in the transmission of human disease is a common characteristic of all the infectious agents included in the genus,

    A. *Bedsonia*
    B. *Brucella*
    C. *Treponema*
    D. *Mycoplasma*
    E. *Rickettsia*

24. Which of the following statements is (are) CORRECT?
    I. A decayed tooth is properly termed a carious tooth.
    II. Dental caries or dental decay is a specific disease which brings about the dissolution and disintegration of the hard structures of the tooth-enamel, cementum, and dentin.
    III. Dental caries is the most widespread disease affecting the human race.
    IV. The incidence of the disease is greatest during childhood and young adulthood.
    V. It attacks deciduous teeth the same as it attacks permanent teeth.
    The CORRECT answer is:

    A. I only
    B. I, II
    C. I, II, III
    D. I, II, III, IV
    E. I, II, III, IV, V

25. Regardless of the method used, sterilization is affected by a number of factors. These are or may be among the following factors listed.
Which are the correct factors?
   I. Cleanliness of material surface being processed
   II. Type of organism to be destroyed
   III. Time the item is exposed to a disinfectant or sterilant
   IV. Steam pressure and temperature (autoclave) used
   V. A clear understanding and observation of the procedure by the user
   VI. Extent of intelligent, painstaking efforts
   VII. Strictness of professional discipline

The CORRECT answer is:

A. I, II, III, IV
B. II, IV, V, VI, VII
C. I, II, IV, VI, VII
D. II, III, IV, V, VI
E. I, II, III, IV, V, VI, VII

25.___

KEY (CORRECT ANSWERS)

1. C
2. B
3. C
4. C
5. C
6. E
7. C
8. A
9. B
10. A

11. B
12. D
13. D
14. D
15. C
16. C
17. E
18. A
19. C
20. D

21. C
22. E
23. E
24. E
25. E

MICROBIOLOGY / PATHOLOGY

EXAMINATION SECTION
TEST 1

DIRECTIONS: Each question or incomplete statement is followed by several suggested answers or completions. Select the one that BEST answers the question or completes the statement. *PRINT THE LETTER OF THE CORRECT ANSWER IN THE SPACE AT THE RIGHT.*

1. Verrucous endocarditis occurs MOST commonly in   1.____

   A. rheumatic fever
   B. tertiary syphilis
   C. staphylococcal septicemia
   D. arteriosclerotic heart disease
   E. subacute bacterial endocarditis

2. Detergents kill bacteria by interfering with the functions of the cell   2.____

   A. wall   B. nucleus   C. capsule
   D. membrane   E. protoplasm

3. Typhus fevers are a result of infection with agents classified as   3.____

   A. fungi   B. viruses   C. bacteria
   D. protozoa   E. rickettsia

4. A fluid containing cells has escaped from the bloodstream into inflamed tissue. The fluid has high specific gravity, a high protein content, and a tendency to coagulate. Such a fluid is PROPERLY termed   4.____

   A. blood   B. plasma   C. exudate
   D. effluvium   E. transudate

5. Herpangina results from an infection caused by   5.____

   A. herpes zoster   B. herpes simplex
   C. Coxiella burnetii   D. psittacosis virus
   E. none of the above

6. Streptococcal infection of the uterus following delivery is known as   6.____

   A. yaws   B. dengue
   C. scarlet fever   D. puerperal fever
   E. relapsing fever

7. The MOST distinguishing characteristics of bacterial genes include   7.____

   A. self-duplication and mutability
   B. haploid and diploid generations
   C. pathogenicity and growth inhibition
   D. protein and phospholipid composition
   E. all of the above

8. The etiology of acute diffuse glomerulonephritis seems to be

   A. circulatory deficiency associated with prolonged shock
   B. bacteremia with localization of organisms in kidney tissue
   C. injury of flomeruli by exogenous inorganic toxins
   D. degenerative changes induced by sclerotic alterations of blood vessels
   E. allergic reaction of glomerular and vascular tissue to beta-hemolytic streptococcal products

9. Lecithinases are produced by

   A. Bacillus anthracis
   B. Corynebacterium diphtheriae
   C. Mycobacterium tuberculosis
   D. Salmonella schottmuelleri
   E. Clostridium perfringens (typhi)

10. The sudden obstruction of some part of the vascular system through the impaction of undissolved material carried there by the blood current is known as

    A. embolism   B. infection   C. infarction
    D. thrombosis   E. organization

11. The FINAL step in the repair of an extensive lesion or wound is the process of

    A. granulation   B. amalgamation   C. condensation
    D. organization   E. cicatrization

12. Which of the following is TRUE of hepatitis B and tuberculosis?

    A. Both are easily detected in dental patients.
    B. The causative organisms appear to be sensitive to most disinfectants.
    C. Both have long incubation periods during which they may be contagious.
    D. Undiagnosed carriers present no problem of cross infection to the dentist and his patients.
    E. Neither can produce a debilitating infection with present therapeutic methods.

13. The class of immunoglobulin MOST abundant in saliva is

    A. IgA   B. IgD   C. IgE   D. IgG   E. IgM

14. Which of the following organisms is associated with thrush?

    A. Candida albicans   B. Proteus vulgaris
    C. Borrelia vincentii   D. Fusobacterium fusiforme
    E. Streptococcus salivarius

15. Which of the following diseases is caused by rickettsia?

    A. San Joaquin fever   B. Typhoid fever
    C. Yellow fever   D. Q fever
    E. Dengue

16. Which of the following skeletal diseases are HEREDITARY in nature?
    I. Achondroplasia
    II. Polyostotic fibrous dysplasia
    III. Cleidocranial dysostosis
    IV. Osteopetrosis
    V. Paget's disease
    The CORRECT answer is:

    A. I, II, III
    B. I, III, IV
    C. I, III, V
    D. I, V
    E. All of the above
    F. None of the above

17. Secondary amyloidosis is seen MOST commonly as a complication of which of the following diseases?

    A. Rabies
    B. Tuberculosis
    C. Secondary lues
    D. Staphylococcal enterocolitis

18. Which of the following protozoans GENERALLY contain species which may live in the oral cavity without apparently causing disease?
    I. Entamoeba
    II. Plasmodium
    III. Giardia
    IV. Trypanosoma
    V. Leishmania
    VI. Balantidium
    VII. Trichomonas
    The CORRECT answer is:

    A. I, II
    B. III, IV
    C. I, V
    D. II, VI
    E. I, VII

19. What is the MOST common site of primary squamous cell carcinoma in women?

    A. Lower lip
    B. Stomach
    C. Breast
    D. Cervix uteri
    E. Lung

20. Each of the following relates to infection with the herpesvirus hominis group EXCEPT

    A. acute gingivostomatitis
    B. keratoconjunctivitis
    C. verruca vulgaris
    D. latency

21. Tumors of which of the sites listed below have a propensity to metastasize to bone?

    A. Testicle and ovary
    B. Brain and nerve tissue
    C. Adrenal cortex and spleen
    D. Tongue and palate
    E. Prostate and breast

22. All of the following are components of the body's nonspecific defense mechanism EXCEPT

    A. fibrinolysin   B. complement   C. interferon
    D. properdin   E. lysozyme

23. What name is given to the condition in which tumor cells revert to a more primitive, embryonic, or undifferentiated form with an increased capacity for reproduction and a decreased functional capacity?

    A. Anaplasia   B. Neoplasia
    C. Hypoplasia   D. Metaplasia

24. All of the following organisms are among the indigenous flora of man EXCEPT

    A. Escherichia coli   B. Shigella flexneri
    C. Streptococcus mitis   D. Streptococcus faecalis
    E. Diplococcus pneumoniae

25. Which of the following may be found in latent infection in the majority of the human population?

    _____ virus.

    A. Mumps   B. Varicella
    C. Foot-and-mouth   D. Herpes simplex
    E. Newcastle disease

KEY (CORRECT ANSWERS)

1. A
2. D
3. E
4. C
5. E

6. D
7. A
8. E
9. E
10. A

11. E
12. C
13. A
14. A
15. D

16. B
17. B
18. E
19. D
20. C

21. E
22. A
23. A
24. B
25. D

TEST 2

DIRECTIONS: Each question or incomplete statement is followed by several suggested answers or completions. Select the one that BEST answers the question or completes the statement. *PRINT THE LETTER OF THE CORRECT ANSWER IN THE SPACE AT THE RIGHT.*

1. Leukocytosis is apt to be present in which of the following conditions? 1.____
    I. Acute abscess
    II. Agranulocytosis
    III. Osteomyelitis
    IV. Leukoplakia
    V. Leukopenia
    The CORRECT answer is:

    A. I, II   B. I, III   C. II, III
    D. III, V   E. IV, V

2. The antigen used in the tuberculin test is 2.____
    I. a purified protein derived from the tubercle bacillus
    II. a sterile filtrate prepared from a culture of tubercle bacilli
    III. a suspension of heat-killed avian tubercle bacilli
    IV. a suspension of viable human tubercle bacilli
    V. the Calmette-Guerin bacillus
    The CORRECT answer is:

    A. I or II   B. I or III   C. II or III
    D. II or IV   E. II or V

3. Dystrophic calcification may be expected in 3.____
    I. atheromas
    II. hyperparathyroidism
    III. hypervitaminosis D
    IV. tuberculous necrosis
    V. calcinosis
    The CORRECT answer is:

    A. I, II   B. I, IV   C. I, V
    D. II, III   E. III, IV   F. IV, V

4. Shock is a condition which OFTEN includes 4.____
    I. tachycardia
    II. feeble pulse
    III. cerebral anoxia
    IV. visceral hyperemia
    V. low blood pressure
    VI. hemoglobinuric nephrosis
    The CORRECT answer is:

    A. II, III, IV   B. I, V, VI
    C. III, V, VI   D. All of the above

5. The Epstein-Barr (EB) virus is a herpes-type virus (HTV) that has been recovered from
   I. Burkitt's lymphona tissue
   II. in human mammary cancer
   III. patients with nasopharyngeal carcinoma
   IV. patients with infectious mononucleosis
   V. cases of herpangina

   The CORRECT answer is:

   A. I, II, V
   B. I, III, IV
   C. II, IV
   D. III *only*
   E. IV, V

6. When horse serum is injected intravenously into a rabbit, and again into the skin 2 or 3 weeks later, a necrotizing reaction occurs at the site of the second injection.
   This is known as

   A. the Prausnitz-Kustner reaction
   B. serum sickness
   C. anaphylaxis
   D. the Arthus phenomenon
   E. atopy

7. Respiratory inflammation is a characteristic of
   I. measles
   II. yellow fever
   III. molluscum contagiosum
   IV. adenovirus
   V. influenza

   The CORRECT answer

   A. I, II, III
   B. I, III, IV
   C. I, IV, V
   D. II, III, V
   E. II, IV, V
   F. All of the above

8. Cloudy swelling of various organs is a common finding at autopsy. Its occurrence

   A. is of little practical diagnostic importance
   B. assists in evaluation of the nutritional status of the organ involved
   C. is useful in identifying certain infections
   D. proves only that circulation was deficient

9. Heart-failure cells are

   A. Aschoff's giant cells
   B. Anitschkow's myocytes
   C. hypertrophic myocardial fibers
   D. hemosiderin-laden macrophages in alveoli

10. The lines of Zahn are found in a(n)

    A. infarct
    B. calcified mass
    C. recent thrombus
    D. postmortem clot
    E. organized thrombus

11. Osteomyelitis is MOST commonly associated with

    A. Nocardia asteroides
    B. Borrelia vincentii
    C. Actinomyces bovis
    D. Staphylococcus aureus
    E. Mycobacterium tuberculosis

11.____

12. Bence Jones proteinuria and hyperglobulinemia is characteristic of

    A. multiple myeloma   B. Hodgkin's disease
    C. monocytic leukemia   D. reticulum cell sarcoma
    E. giant follicle lymphoma

12.____

13. Cotton, fabric material, paper, plastic, rubber, and other heat-sensitive materials may be sterilized without destruction by means of

    A. dry heat
    B. boiling water
    C. ethylene oxide
    D. quaternary ammonium compounds

13.____

14. Use of vaccines for preventing clinical symptoms after introduction of the virus is MOST likely to be effective against

    A. rabies   B. influenza
    C. poliomyelitis   D. herpes zoster
    E. serum hepatitis

14.____

15. The neoplasm to which the endocrine effect of hypertension is attributed is

    A. fetal adenoma of thyroid
    B. eosinophilic adenoma
    C. pheochromocytoma
    D. arrhenoblastoma
    E. none of the above

15.____

16. Abscess formation is PARTICULARLY characteristic of _____ infection.

    A. viral   B. rickettsial
    C. streptococcal   D. staphylococcal

16.____

17. The MOST active cellular structure in controlling the intake of solutions into bacteria is the

    A. capsule   B. flagella
    C. cell wall   D. cytoplasmic membrane

17.____

18. Amebiasis, malaria, and trypanosomiasis are ALL caused by

    A. viruses   B. bacteria   C. spirochetes
    D. protozoa   E. mycoplasma

18.____

19. Lactobacilli were often named among bacteria able to initiate dental caries because they are

    A. abundant in calculus
    B. both acidogenic and aciduric
    C. capable of surviving without nutrients
    D. the only acid-forming bacteria in the mouth
    E. isolated from mouths with rampant dental decay only

20. A biopsy report of a nodule in the palate reads as follows: *A central area of caseous necrosis was noted with cluster of epithelioid cells and giant cells surrounded by a peripheral zone of lymphocytes.*
    The associated condition is MOST likely

    A. an abscess   B. syphilis
    C. tuberculosis   D. Hodgkin's disease
    E. mycotic infection

21. Organisms reproducing mainly by spore formation, which elaborate no endotoxin and grow on Sabouraud's media, are

    A. fungi   B. bacteria   C. mycoplasma
    D. rickettsia   E. spirochetes

22. Carbon tetrachloride is an extremely toxic substance when ingested or inhaled because it COMMONLY produces

    A. agranulocytosis
    B. necrosis of the liver
    C. fatty infiltration of the heart
    D. degenerative changes of the basal ganglia of the brain

23. Each of the following may be indicative of congenital syphilis EXCEPT

    A. eighth nerve deafness
    B. interstitial keratitis
    C. notching of central incisors
    D. saddle deformity of the nose
    E. radiating scars about the mouth
    F. pulmonary hyaline membrane formation

24. Lysozyme is a(n)

    A. histamine-producing mast cell
    B. antibody that facilitates phagocytosis
    C. enzyme found in high concentration in tears and saliva
    D. class of intracellular vesicles containing a number of hydrolytic enzymes
    E. substance capable of causing normal cells to acquire neoplastic characteristics

25. Tularemia is transmitted by
    A. the bite of rat lice
    B. mosquito bites
    C. direct contact with convalescent patients
    D. droplet transmission
    E. the bite of infected flies and ticks

25.____

KEY (CORRECT ANSWERS)

1. B
2. A
3. B
4. D
5. B

6. D
7. C
8. A
9. D
10. C

11. D
12. A
13. C
14. A
15. C

16. D
17. D
18. D
19. B
20. C

21. A
22. B
23. F
24. C
25. E

STERILANTS AND DISINFECTANTS IN HEALTHCARE FACILITIES

In a healthcare setting, it is essential to be able to control infectious organisms. Sterilants and disinfectants are important tools for meeting that need. But because they are necessarily toxic to living organisms, sterilants and disinfectants must be handled carefully, and their associated wastes must be managed properly, to avoid causing unintentional harm as they fulfill their intended function. These page provide an introduction to sterilants and disinfectants in common use, and include information on proper handling and disposal, and on available alternatives.

The information presented below applies primarily to sterilizing and disinfecting medical devices and other items that may contact patients.

- Properties
- Risks
- Compliance requirements
- Alternatives
- Disposal of sterilant and disinfectant wastes

Properties

Sterilants and disinfectants kill living organisms. They need that essential property to perform their basic function. But "desirable" organisms (like us, presumably), and "undesirable" organisms, like disease-causing pathogens, are not that different at the cellular level, where their basic metabolic processes are concerned. If a substance is toxic to pathogens, chances are it will also be harmful to other organisms.

While all sterilants and disinfectants are toxic to some degree, some have greater killing power than others. High toxicity is an advantage in critical applications, where the risk of infection must be reduced to the lowest possible level. But the greater effectiveness of highly toxic materials comes at a price:

- the risk of harm to staff and patients through inadvertent exposure will be greater
- the disposal of wastes from disinfection processes may become more difficult and costly

Healthcare professionals have developed two interrelated classification systems to help determine appropriate infection control materials for various clinical situations. One system is concerned with classifying **levels of infection risk** -- in other words, with providing "how clean is clean?" guidelines based on plausible exposure risks. The other system is concerned with classifying **levels of effective potency** of disinfection materials. Using the two systems, you can match the material with the need, and ensure a safe level of infection control without overkill -- i.e. without overusing materials that pose needless risks of their own, and increase your costs as well.

Categories of Infection Risk

According to one commonly used scheme, infection risk situations are divided into three categories:

- **Critical:** contact directly with internal fluids, such as with circulating blood though blood vessel walls, or contact directly with tissues through broken skin
- **Semi-critical:** contact with mucous membranes, or contact with broken skin
- **Noncritical:** contact with intact skin

Categories of Effective Potency

Sterilants and disinfectants are distinguished according to the degree to which they can be expected to destroy the organisms they contact:

- **Sterilants** are capable of completely eliminating or destroying all forms of microbial life, including spores.
- **Disinfectants** form a less absolute category -- they will destroy some, but not necessarily all organisms. The category is further divided into subcategories, as follows:
    - **High-level disinfectants** - destroy all microorganisms, with the exception of high numbers of bacterial spores.
    - **Intermediate-level disinfectants** - inactivate even resistant organisms such as *Mycobacterium* tuberculosis, as well as vegetative bacteria, most viruses, and most fungi, but do not necessarily kill bacterial spores.
    - **Low-level disinfectants** - kill most bacteria, some viruses, and some fungi, but cannot be relied on to kill resistant microorganisms such as tubercle bacilli or bacterial spores. (Source: APIC.)

Choosing the appropriate material to match risk with potency

- Any objects or materials used where the risk of infection is **critical** should be absolutely sterile.
- For **semi-critical** risk situations, either a high-level or a medium-level disinfectant may be appropriate, depending on the type of exposure. For example, a publication from the Association for Professionals in Infection Control and Epidemiology (APIC) recommends high-level disinfectants for devices like laryngoscopes and endoscopes that are inserted deep into body cavities, and medium-level disinfectants for less intrusive devices such as oral or rectal thermometers.
- For **noncritical** risk situations, low-level disinfectants may be adequate.

The most widely used sterilants and disinfectants in healthcare facilities are:

- **Ethylene oxide (EtO).** Hospitals typically use ethylene oxide (EtO) to sterilize moisture- and heat-sensitive instruments. EtO is a hazardous air pollutant (HAP) and the operation of EtO sterilizers is regulated by a National Emission Standard for Hazardous Air Pollutants (for guidance on how to comply see: EPA guidance document Summary of Regulations Controlling Air Emissions from the Hospital Sterilizers Using Ethylene Oxide).
- **Glutaraldehyde.** Glutaraldehyde is a high-level disinfectant most frequently used as a disinfectant for heat-sensitive equipment such as dialysis instruments, surgical

instruments, suction bottles, bronchoscopes, endoscopes, and ear, nose, and throat instruments. Glutaraldehyde is also used as a tissue fixative in histology and pathology laboratories and as a hardening agent in the development of x-rays. Glutaraldehyde products are marketed under a variety of brand names and are available in a variety of concentrations (solutions range in concentration from 2.4 – 3.4%), with and without surfactants.

Both of these materials have been found to cause potential problems for facility staff and for any other individuals who may be exposed to them (see the following section). Alternatives are available for most applications (see the Alternatives section below).

Note that there are also non-chemical methods of sterilizing and disinfecting that may be suitable in some cases:

- Some methods rely on high heat and pressure, such as the conditions obtainable in an autoclave. Since boiling in water is not sufficient for sterilization -- some particularly hardy spores can survive exposure to the temperature at which water boils under normal atmospheric pressure -- more drastic conditions are needed to sterilize without the use of biotoxic chemicals. Autoclaves are enclosed chambers that operate under increased pressure, allowing water to remain liquid at temperatures well above its normal boiling point. This can provide a very effective sterilization environment. However, autoclaving is not an option for heat sensitive equipment.
- Radiation can also be used for sterilizing and disinfecting, but considering its own well-known suite of problems, it would not generally be considered a preferable alternative to chemical methods from an environmental and safety standpoint.

Risks

(Note -- this section deals with the risks involved in using and disposing of the most commonly used sterilants and disinfectants. The risks associated with infection are surveyed in the previous section.)

Ethylene oxide (EtO) poses several health hazards requiring special handling and disposal of the chemical, and training in its use. It is identified by the National Toxicology Program as a known human carcinogen and has several other acute and chronic health effects. Ethylene oxide:

- can cause nausea, vomiting, and neurological disorders
- in solution, can severely irritate and burn the skin, eyes, and lungs
- acts as a probable teratogen, and may pose reproductive hazards
- may damage the central nervous system, liver, and kidneys, or cause cataracts
- is extremely reactive and flammable, increasing the risk of chemical accidents that could injure hospital employees and patients

(Source: Replacing Ethylene Oxide and Glutaraldehyde, USEPA)

Glutaraldehyde is not a human carcinogen. However, several health effects have been reported among healthcare workers exposed to glutaraldehyde:

- asthma, and breathing difficulties

- burning eyes and conjunctivitis
- headaches
- nosebleed, irritation, sneezing, and wheezing
- hives
- nausea
- rashes and allergic dermatitis
- staining of the hands
- throat and lung irritation

(Source: Glutaraldehyde: Occupational Hazards in Hospitals, CDC)

Compliance requirements

Several Occupational Safety and Health Administration (OSHA) regulations relate to sterilants and disinfectants:

- OSHA has established a permissible exposure limit (PEL) standard for ethylene oxide of 1 ppm in air as an 8 hour time weighted average, and 5 ppm over any 15 minute sampling period.
- OSHA's Hazard Communication Standard (HazCom), requires that information concerning any associated health or physical hazards be transmitted to employees via comprehensive hazard communication programs (Go to HERC HazCom page). The programs must include:
    - **Written Program.** A written that meets the requirements of the Hazard Communication Standard (HazCom).
    - **Labels.** In-plant containers of hazardous chemicals must be labeled, tagged, or marked with the identity of the material and appropriate hazard warnings.
    - **Material Safety Data Sheets.** Employers must have an MSDS for each hazardous chemical which they use and MSDSs must be readily accessible to employees when they are in their work areas during their workshifts.
    - **Employee Information and Training.** Each employee who may be "exposed" to hazardous chemicals when working must be provided information and be trained prior to initial assignment to work with a hazardous chemical, and whenever the hazard changes.
- Depending on the ingredients contained in a sterilant or disinfectant and its manner of use, employee protection may be required, including:
    - ventilation controls
    - personal protective equipment
    - clothing or gloves

and other applicable precautions. This assessment should be made by the employer, again, based on the unique conditions of use of the product at that establishment.

- Where the eyes or body of any person may be exposed to injurious corrosive materials, **employers must provide** suitable mechanisms for quick drenching or flushing of the eyes and body within the work area for immediate emergency use [1910.151(c)].

Certain Environmental Protection Agency (EPA) regulations may also apply to sterilants and disinfectants:

- On December 20, 2007, the EPA issued nationwide standards (NESHAP Subpart WWWWW) to reduce emissions of ethylene oxide (EtO) from hospital sterilizers. This regulation requires hospitals to implement a management practice to reduce ethylene oxide emissions by sterilizing full loads to the extent practicable. Hospitals which route ethylene oxide to a control device are in compliance with the rule requirements. Existing sources must be in compliance by December 29, 2008. New sources (construction after Nov. 6, 2006) must be in compliance at the time of startup. Affected hospitals must submit a Notification of Compliance Status (INOCS) within 180 days after their compliance date (for guidance on how to comply see: EPA guidance document Summary of Regulations Controlling Air Emissions from the Hospital Sterilizers Using Ethylene Oxide).
- The Federal Insecticide, Fungicide and Rodenticide Act (FIFRA) provides EPA with the authority to oversee the registration, distribution, sale and use of pesticides. FIFRA applies to all types of pesticides, including antimicrobials, which includes sterilants, disinfectants and other cleaning compounds that are intended to control microorganisms on surfaces. FIFRA requires users of products to follow the labeling directions on each product explicitly. (go to FIFRA page).
- Discarded sterilants and disinfectants may be a hazardous waste due to their corrosiveness, flammability, toxicity, or reactivity. For information on how to properly identify your hazardous waste, please see HERC's Hazardous Waste Determination page. You should also check the HERC Hazardous Waste State Resource Locator page for your state for links to any state-specific variations on the federal rules that may apply to you.

Some sterilants and disinfectants are considered hazardous wastes, and are regulated under RCRA (see below).

A brief summary of which federal agency plays what role in the regulation of sterilants and disinfectants can be found in a document from the Centers for Disease Control.

Alternatives

Because of the health and environmental hazards associated with glutaraldehyde and ethylene oxide, various alternatives have been investigated. This section lists several sterilants and high level disinfectants that have been cleared by the Food and Drug Administration (FDA) for processing reusable medical and dental devices along with specific references to some commercially available products.

The list is provided for your convenience, and is not intended to provide specific recommendations. In general, when selecting an alternative, you should choose a disinfectant that is sufficiently effective, but is the least toxic to employees and the environment.

Here are a few general observations.

- Disinfectants that act by generating active forms of oxygen, such as hydrogen peroxide or peracetic acid, typically create fewer by-products than compounds relying on other active elements, such as chlorine or the form of nitrogen found in quaternary amine compounds. This means fewer toxins finding their way to the sewer.
- Hydrogen peroxide and peracetic acid are less easily inactivated by other, noninfectious organic matter than some of the non-oxygen disinfectants.

- Hydrogen peroxide and peracetic acid can be effective against a broader range of infectious agents than some of the other alternatives.

Under any circumstances, when alternatives sterilants and disinfectants are to be used on a medical device, you should check with the original equipment manufacturer for any specific warranty restrictions on the use of specific materials or methods of disinfection.

Hydrogen peroxide provides high level disinfection in 30 minutes at 20 degrees Celsius. Although the FDA has approved products containing 7.5% hydrogen peroxide as a high-level disinfectant/sterilant, it has not been found to be compatible with all flexible gastrointestinal endoscopes (e.g., Olympus, Pentax or Fujinon). Available products include:

- **Sporox™ Sterilizing & Disinfection Solution,** Sultan Chemists, (7.5% hydrogen peroxide)
- Sterrad™ Sterilization Systems, Johnson & Johnson, (hydrogen peroxide plasma)

Peracetic acid is part of the family of peryoxygen compounds. A concentration of 0.2% peracetic acid is rapidly active against all microorganisms including bacterial spores, and is effective in the presence of organic matter. It has proved to be an acceptable alternative to EtO. FDA cleared products include:

- **STERIS 20™ Sterilant** (*Cleared for use with the STERIS System 1™ Processor only.*), STERIS™ Corporation, **0.2% peracetic acid.**

However, you should note that in some instances, manufacturers have not yet approved the use of EtO alternatives for sterilization of their products. Such limitations vary by vendor and are not specific to one instrument or medical device product type. For example, one typical hospital has investigated EtO alternatives, but still requires the use of EtO on the following five instruments:

- angioscopes
- choledocoscopes
- surgiscopes
- bone flaps
- hysterectoscopes.

(Source: Replacing Ethylene Oxide and Glutaraldehyde, USEPA).

Peracetic Acid-Hydrogen Peroxide mixtures. Although the FDA has approved products containing 0.08% Peracetic Acid/1% Hydrogen Peroxide as a high-level disinfectant/sterilant, it has not been found to be compatible with flexible gastrointestinal endoscopes manufactured by Olympus, Pentax or Fujinon. FDA cleared products include:

- **Acecide™ High Level Disinfectant and Sterilant,** Minntech Corp., 8.3% hydrogen peroxide 7.0% peracetic acid,
- **EndoSpor™ Plus Sterilizing and Disinfecting Solution,** Cottrell Limited, 7.35% hydrogen peroxide 0.23% peracetic acid
- **Peract™ 20 Liquid Sterilant/Disinfectant,** Minntech Corp., 1.0% hydrogen peroxide, 0.08% peracetic acid

Hypochlorite has FDA clearance for high level disinfection in 10 minutes at 25 degrees Celsius. FDA cleared products include:

- **Sterilox Liquid High Level Disinfectant System,** Sterilox, Technologies, Inc., hypochlorite and hypochlorous acid, 650-675 ppm active free chlorine.

Ortho-phthalaldehyde (OPA) is chemically related to glutaraldehyde. According to the Michigan Health and Hospital Association (MHA), the disinfecting mechanism of OPA is thought to be similar to glutaraldehyde and is based on the powerful binding of the aldehyde to the outer cell wall of contaminant organisms. A notable difference between the two commercial disinfectants is the percent of active ingredient in each product. Commercial OPA-based disinfecting products contain only 0.55% of the active ingredient, while most glutaraldehyde-based disinfecting products contain 2.4 to 3.2% active ingredient – 5 to 7 times that of OPA products. is a widely used glutaraldehyde alternative. Its potential benefits include:

- lower inhalation exposure risk,
- reduced disinfecting time (12 minutes vs. APIC-approved 20 minute disinfection time and FDA-approved 45 minute disinfecting time for Cidex),
- solution is approved for use in almost all of their equipment without negating the warranty, and
- cost is significantly less than installing a more substantial ventilation system to minimize respiratory irritation from using glutaraldehyde.

Ortho-phthalaldehyde is a clear blue solution with little odor. It is a potential irritant of eyes, skin, nose and other tissues resulting in symptoms such as stinging, excessive tearing, coughing and sneezing. It is a potential skin and respiratory sensitizer that may cause dermatitis with prolonged or repeated contact and may aggravate pre-existing bronchitis or asthma. In addition, the product stains proteins on surfaces to gray/black. Although OPA may pose similar occupational hazards to glutaraldehyde, the risk is significantly reduced due to the low percentage of OPA and relatively low vapor pressure of OPA-based commercial products. OPA does not currently have a recommended exposure limit; however, vendors recommend that similar protective equipment be used, including gloves and goggles. (Source: Replacing Ethylene Oxide and Glutaraldehyde, USEPA). FDA cleared products include:

- **Cidex OPA Concentrate,** Advanced Sterilization Products, (5.75% *ortho*-phthalaldehyde)
- **Cidex OPA Solution,** Advanced Sterilization Products, (0.55% *ortho*-phthalaldehyde)

Disposal of sterilant and disinfectant wastes

Unused disinfectant concentrates may be considered hazardous wastes in some cases. If so, they need to be managed under a particular set of rules (RCRA). You should also to check to see if the end product being used (i.e. the product after dilution) also needs to be managed under RCRA.

Here are a few considerations:

- If the sole active ingredient of a sterilant or disinfectant is a P or U-listed waste, the product itself must be managed as a hazardous waste. (This information should be

available on the Material Safety Data Sheet (MSDS) that your supplier can provide for the product.)
- A sterilant or disinfectant might also have to be considered a <u>characteristic hazardous waste</u> due to:
    - <u>corrosivity</u>: It is important to check the pH level of the product. Many products have pHs higher than 11 or lower than 2. A sterilant or disinfectant product may be considered hazardous if it has a pH of less than 2 or greater than 12.5. This information can be determined form the MSDS under the "Physical Data" category.
    - <u>toxicity</u>
    - <u>reactivity</u>

See the <u>Hazardous Waste Determination page</u> for more background information on this topic.

Some solutions can be disposed of to the sanitary sewer if the local POTW permits it. You are strongly advised to check with your POTW to determine what wastewater discharges of sterilants and disinfectants are acceptable.

A note on the disposal of ortho-phthalaldehyde (OPA)-containing products: Due to its toxicity, California legislation deemed Cidex OPA a hazardous waste beginning January 1, 2001. However, this legislation exempts healthcare facilities from tiered permitting regulatory requirements when treating Cidex OPA with glycine on site to render it a non hazardous waste. Note also that if local publicly owned treatment works (POTWs) or sewer agencies have other prohibitions against sewerage of aldehydes, facilities must seek approval for this process as well. (Source: <u>Replacing Ethylene Oxide and Glutaraldehyde</u>, USEPA)

HOSPITAL STERILIZERS.

Many hospitals have already moved away from using EtO sterilization to other methods. Since EtO was recognized as a known human carcinogen in 1994, the estimated total tonnage of EtO used by U.S. hospitals has dropped from about 1000 tons per year to approximately 135 tons per year in 2005.

A number of other sterilization technologies exist. Many of these can replace some but not all EtO applications, so a hospital's sterilization strategy may include two or more options. These include steam, chemical sterilization with less-toxic processes such as sonic sterilization, gas plasma, electron beam, microwave, or hydrogen peroxide.

One hospital, for example, estimates that they have been able to reduce EtO use by 60-70%, but that EtO is still used, with proper safety precautions for angioscopes, choledocoscopes, surgiiscopes, bone flaps, and hysterectoscopes.

If EtO is still used for some purposes, the following practices will reduce hazardous emissions and risk to employees and patients.

- Sterilize full loads to the extent practical.
- Use self-contained scrubbers, combustion units, or gas collection to prevent EtO from escaping into the air.
- Recover and dispose of EtO as dangerous waste.
- Filter air and dispose of spent filters as dangerous waste.
- EtO may be manufactured with another gas as a carrier. Choose EtO with less-toxic carriers such as carbon dioxide or 100% ethylene oxide. Prior to the ban on chlorofluorocarbons, Freon was a carrier gas, which added to the toxic emissions. Note that the carrier gas doesn't add to the sterilization efficacy so the concentration of EtO has to be sufficient for proper sterilization.

Alternative Sterilization Options: Advantages and Disadvantages

Some available alternative sterilization options include the following list. Potential pros and cons are listed in the tables below.

- Plasma phase hydrogen peroxide
- Peracetic acid
- Ozone
- Ionizing radiation
- Steam or dry heat autoclaves
- Disposable single use devices (SUD)
- Reprocessed/sterilized SUDs
- Chlorine Dioxide (ClO2)
- Pulsed light systems

1. Plasma phase hydrogen peroxide

Advantages	Disadvantages
Acceptable alternative in many cases	Some manufacturers haven't approved this method for their devices yet (such as mixed material devices)
Shorter processing time = higher productivity	High initial cost
No utility connection except power	Items must be completely dry
No waste	No paper or liquids
Completely sealed sterilant eliminates contact	
Automated processing	
Small footprint	
Moderate cost per cycle	
Single channel flexible endoscopes can be processed	

2. Peracetic acid

Advantages	Disadvantages
Acceptable alternative in many cases	Some manufacturers haven't approved this method for their devices yet (such as mixed material devices)
Shorter processing time = higher productivity	"Just-in-time" technology; so sterilized items must be removed from the unit and used immediately, which makes it impractical in certain applications
Small footprint	Limitation on types of scopes that can be processed
Closed automated system	Is an irritant and possible problem for asthmatics
	Highly toxic and corrosive substances
	High repair costs

3. Ozone

Advantages	Disadvantages
Devices don't have to be completely dry to process	New untested technology
Large capacity	Can't reprocess flexible endoscopes
Closed automated system	Many materials are incompatible
No toxic waste	Possibility of O2 enriched atmosphere
Water and electricity are the only utilities needed	
Low cost per cycle	
Conditionally approved by the FDA	

4. Ionizing radiation

Advantages	Disadvantages
May be used for product designs and packaging materials that are impermeable to gases as long as they are "transparent" to energy of the wavelengths employed in the sterilization process	

5. Steam or dry heat autoclaves

Advantages	Disadvantages
Good alternative for many traditional surgical instruments	High pressure and high temperature makes this alternative unsuitable for products that are sensitive to heat, like mixed media instruments, rubber, plastics, glass and those affected by the corrosive and dielectric effects of steam
Comparable to chemiclaves without the hazardous waste	Disposal of wastewater may be subject to state regulation

6. Disposable single use devices (SUD's)

Advantages	Disadvantages
Eliminates need to sterilize devices	Creates direct increase in solid and hazardous waste
Eliminates internal costs and workload	Higher Cost

7. Reprocessed/sterilized SUD's

Advantages	Disadvantages
Outside provider takes the responsibility of sterilization. Eliminates internal costs and workload	Dependant on reliability of vendor
Reduces solid and hazardous waste	May not reduce EtO if reprocessor is using it

8. Chlorine Dioxide (ClO2)

Advantages	Disadvantages
No significant levels of residual sterilant on product	Can't be safely stored under pressure for transport and subsequent use since it is explosive in liquid form
Not flammable in gaseous systems	Unstable and corrosive in liquid form
Used for contact lenses and foil suture packages	Concentration rapidly diminishes when in liquid form
When used with stabilizing agents, liquid form is used for fiber-optic endoscopes	

9. Pulsed light systems

Advantages	Disadvantages
Reported to be effective killing micro-organisms including spores	Effectiveness depends on light access to surface, so porous surfaces, turbid liquids and non-transparent materials are not applicable
Low costs around one cent per square meter sterilized	Possible degradation of surface of opaque materials

Specific sterilization options vary by vendor and by type of device. Some of the characteristics to consider are the following:

- Processing time
- Up front cost
- Ongoing costs for supplies
- Length of time devices remain sterile
- Residue requiring special handling or not
- How wastes can be neutralized
- Types of devices accommodated; soft metals, plastics, packaging

For a detailed list with pros and cons by vendor name brands, see the Vendors List: Less Hazardous Products and Waste Management in the link to the Best Management Practices for Hospital Waste from the Washington Department of Ecology,

Keep the following tips in mind when choosing a vendor:

- Ask for least toxic products available. Ask if they have products that do not become dangerous waste when spent or are recyclable.
- Ask vendors for customer references (name, phone and address) that use the product or service in the same manner you will be using it. Contact these customers and ask for their opinion of the product or service. Ask the customers what they like or don't like about the product or service.
- Contact your state ecology office for vendor's compliance history.
- Get a number of bids and compare. Choose your vendors carefully; consider reliability as well as costs.
- Test the product or service to see if it satisfies your requirements prior to making a commitment to purchase the product or use the service.
- Ask if the product or service is "drop in" prior to product purchase or service use or if new equipment will be necessary. Ask to see total costs or fees associated with the product or service.
- Whenever possible, require your waste contractor to pick-up only on request. In your contract with your waste hauler, have it clearly written that they will only pick up on request. Keep wastes separate, if necessary. Don't over-accumulate wastes. Fill all containers prior to disposal. Keep containers closed, labeled and in good condition and stored in secondary containment, when necessary.
- Know the fate of your waste. You are ultimately responsible for the proper disposal of your waste.

HEALTHCARE WIDE HAZARDS
GLUTERALDEHYDE

Potential Hazard

Exposure of employees to glutaraldehyde. Glutaraldehyde is a toxic chemical that is used as a cold sterilant to disinfect and clean heat-sensitive medical, surgical and dental equipment. It is found in products such as Cidex, Aldesen, Hospex, Sporicidin, Omnicide, Matricide, Wavicide and others. Glutaraldehyde is also used as a tissue fixative in histology and pathology labs and as a hardening agent in the development of x-rays.

The National Institute for Occupational Safety and Health (NIOSH) suggests ways in which health care workers may be exposed to glutaraldehyde including:
- Hospital staff who work in areas with a cold sterilizing procedure that uses glutaraldehyde (e.g., gastroenterology or cardiology departments).

- Hospital staff who work in operating rooms, dialysis departments, endoscopy units, and intensive care units, where glutaraldehyde formulations are used in infection control procedures.

- Central Supply workers who use glutaraldehyde as a sterilant.

- Research Technicians, researchers, and pharmacy personnel who either prepare the alkaline solutions or fix tissues in histology and pathology labs.

- Laboratory workers who sterilize bench tops with glutaraldehyde solutions.

- Workers who develop x-rays.

Glutaraldehyde is used in a limited number of applications, rather than as a general disinfectant. Specific applications include use as a disinfecting agent for respiratory therapy equipment, bronchoscopes, physical therapy whirlpool tubs, surgical instruments, anesthesia equipment parts, x-ray tabletops, dialyzers, and dialysis treatment equipment (Air contaminants, Section 7 - VII. Feasibility and Regulatory Analyses).

Health effects of glutaraldehyde exposure include:
- **Short term (acute) effects:** Contact with glutaraldehyde liquid and vapor can severely irritate the eyes, and at higher concentrations burns the skin. Breathing glutaraldehyde can irritate the nose, throat, and respiratory tract, causing coughing and wheezing, nausea, headaches, drowsiness, nosebleeds, and dizziness.

- **Long-term (chronic) effects:** Glutaraldehyde is a sensitizer. This means some workers will become very sensitive to glutaraldehyde and have strong reactions if they are exposed to even small amounts. Workers may get sudden asthma attacks with difficult breathing, wheezing, coughing, and tightness in the chest. Prolonged exposure can cause a skin allergy and chronic eczema, and afterwards, exposure to small amounts produces severe itching and skin rashes. It has been implicated as a possible cause of occupational asthma.

Possible Solutions

Limit exposure to glutaraldehyde through work practice, engineering controls and personal protective equipment (PPE) including:
- Make sure that rooms in which glutaraldehyde is to be used are well ventilated and large enough to ensure adequate dilution of vapor, with a minimum air exchange rate of 10 air changes per hour.
    - Ideally, install local exhaust ventilation such as properly functioning laboratory fume hoods (capture velocity of at least 100 feet per minute) to control vapor.
    - Keep glutaraldehyde baths under a fume hood where possible.
- Use only enough glutaraldehyde to perform the required disinfecting procedure.
- Store glutaraldehyde in closed containers in well ventilated areas. Air-tight containers are available. Post signs to remind staff to replace lids after using product.
- Use specially designed, mobile, compact, disinfectant soaking stations to facilitate sterilization of heat sensitive equipment such as endoscopes, or GI scopes. These soaking stations provide an enclosed area for sterilizing trays, and remove fumes from glutaraldehyde and other disinfectants.
- Use appropriate PPE covered under [29 CFR 1910.132(a)] including:
    - Use gloves that are impervious to glutaraldehyde such as those made of Butyl Rubber, Nitrile, and Viton®, which have been shown to provide full shift protection from glutaraldehyde.
    - For shorter exposures, you can use gloves made of polyethylene. Do not use Neoprene and PVC gloves because they do not provide adequate protection against glutaraldehyde and may actually absorb it.
    - Do not use latex surgical exam gloves for skin protection against glutaraldehyde, except in situations where only short-term, incidental contact is expected.
    - Wear lab coats, aprons, or gowns made of appropriate materials such as polypropylene to provide additional protection.
    - Wear splash-proof goggles and/or full face shields when working with glutaraldehyde to protect eyes.
- All employees who may be exposed to above the ceiling threshold limit value (TLV) of 0.05 ppm, should use appropriate respirators for glutaraldehyde vapor during routine or emergency work. Respirator requirements are found in the OSHA respiratory protection standard [29 CFR 1910.134]
- Provide eye wash fountains for immediate emergency use [29 CFR 1910.151(c)].
    - Use eye wash fountains and emergency showers if there is skin contact with glutaraldehyde. Flush area with water for at least 15 minutes to remove chemical.
    - Change into clean clothes if clothing becomes contaminated.
- Clean up spills immediately.
    - Refer to ANSI/AAMI [1996] for further information about emergency procedures in the event of a large spill.
- Do not eat, drink, or smoke in any area where glutaraldehyde is handled or stored.

- Use a vacuum or wet method to reduce dust while cleaning up pure glutaraldehyde. Do not dry sweep.

- Use less toxic products if feasible and available, or other processes for sterilization.

- Automate the transfer of pure glutaraldehyde or pump liquid glutaraldehyde from drums or other storage containers to appropriate containers and operations, avoiding exposure to glutaraldehyde by keeping it in a contained process.

- Hazard Communication Standard [29 CFR 1910.1200] requires employers to ensure that the hazards of all chemicals are evaluated and that this information is transmitted to the employees by means of a hazards communication program which includes, labeling, material safety data sheets, and employee training.

Additional Information:
- Best Practices for the Safe Use of Glutaraldehyde in Health Care [261 KB PDF*, 48 pages]. OSHA Publication 3258-08N, (2006).

- OSHA does not currently have a required permissible exposure level (PEL) for glutaraldehyde.
    - The American Conference of Government Industrial Hygienists (ACGIH) has a recommended ceiling Threshold Limit Value (TLV) of 0.05 ppm (parts per million). This represents an airborne concentration that should not be exceeded during any part of the work shift.

    - NIOSH has established a recommended exposure limit of 0.2 ppm for glutaraldehyde vapor from either activated or unactivated solutions. This TLV is based on the irritation threshold in humans.
- Glutaraldehyde Occupational Hazards in Hospitals. US Department of Health Human Services (DHHS), National Institute for Occupational Safety and Health (NIOSH) Publication No. 2001-115, (2001, May).

- Air Contaminants. OSHA Preamble to Final Rules, (1989).
    - Section 7 - VII. Feasibility and Regulatory Analyses
- Use of Latex Surgical Exam Gloves for Protection Against Glutaraldehyde. OSHA Standard Interpretation, (1997, October 3).

- *American National Standards Institute/ Association for the Advancement of Medical Instrumentation (ANSI/AAMI)*
    - *ST58-1996*, Safe Use and Handling of Glutaraldehyde-based Products in Healthcare Facilities

MEDICAL/NURSING SCIENCE
ISOLATION TECHNIQUES AND PROCEDURES

CONTENTS

		Page
A.	Isolation Techniques	1
	Handwashing Techniques	4
	Mask Technique	5
	Gown Technique	6
	Care of Linen	9
	Serving Food with Disposable Dishes	10
	Medications for the Isolated Patient	11
	Care of Body Discharges and Excreta	12
	Terminal Disinfection	13
B.	Isolation Procedures for Specific Communicable Diseases	14

MEDICAL/NURSING SCIENCE
ISOLATION TECHNIQUES AND PROCEDURES
A. ISOLATION TECHNIQUES

PURPOSE

To prevent transmission of infection from the patient to other persons.
To prevent reinfection of the patient.

PREPARATION OF THE UNIT WITH HANDWASHING FACILITIES
(Sink and running water)

Outside unit:

1. Place "ISOLATION" sign with listed necessary precautions at entrance.
2. Stock locker with disposable or clean gowns, disposable or clean masks and disposable gloves, if applicable.

Inside the Patient's Room:

1. Ascertain that the following is in the room:
   *a. Hand washing unit:
      1. Paper towels in towel dispenser over sink.
      2. Soap in soap dispenser which is foot operated.
      3. Step-on can lined with water proof bag for used paper towels.
      4. Linen hamper.

   b. At the bedside:
      1. Overbed table, chair, bedside locker, overhead bed lamp.
      2. Water pitcher and glass.
      3. Drinking tube if necessary.
      4. Paper bag.
      5. Towel and washcloth.
      6. Facial tissues.
      7. Call bell or signal cord.
      8. Clock.
      9. Thermometer in disinfectant solution.

*If anteroom is provided between corridor and patient's room, the handwashing unit should be located here.

   c. In the bedside locker:
      1. Toilet articles.
      2. Bath Basin.
      3. Curved Basin.
      4. Bedpan, urinal, paper covers.
      5. Toilet tissue.
      6. Necessary linen.

IMPROVISED ISOLATION TECHNIQUE

Preparation of unit when running water and hand-washing facilities are not available:

1. <u>Outside the patient's unit:</u>
    a) Place Isolation sign with listed necessary precautions at entrance.
    b) Stock locker with clean or disposable gowns, clean or disposable masks, and disposable gloves if applicable.

2. <u>Inside the patient's unit:</u>
    *a. Hand cleansing unit
        1. Container of prepackaged disinfectant towelettes on small table at room entrance.
        2. Paper towels
        3. Step-on can or waste paper basket with waxed paper bag inside for used towels.
        4. Linen hamper.

    b. At the Bedside:
        1. Overbed table, chair, bedside locker, overhead bed lamp.
        2. Water pitcher and glass.
        3. Drinking tube if necessary.
        4. Paper bag.
        5. Towel and washcloth.
        6. Facial tissues.
        7. Call bell or signal cord.
        8. Clock.
        9. Thermometer in disinfectant solution.

*The principle of handwashing is primarily that of mechanical removal of dirt, microorganism, etc., by sudsing, friction, and flushing with running water. It is important; therefore, that hands be washed at the nearest sink immediately after leaving the isolation unit described above.

    c. In the bedside locker:
        1. Toilet articles.
        2. Bath Basin.
        3. Curved basin.
        4. Bedpan, urinal, paper covers.
        5. Toilet tissue.
        6. Necessary linen.

POINTS TO EMPHASIZE

1. Units selected for isolated patients should have a sink with running water and toilet facilities when possible.
2. All personnel must be aware of the extent of isolation zones.
3. Patients capable of being instructed should be made aware of the isolation areas and the need for isolation.
4. Handwashing unit, whether located within the patient's room or in the anteroom, should be considered a clean area. Preferably, the water spigots and soap dispensers should be operated by knee or foot controls.
5. All personnel should wash hands again under running water after leaving an isolation unit.
6. Ambulatory patients should be instructed not to enter handwashing and isolation areas.
7. Visitors should be kept to a minimum and assisted in gowning and ungowning when entering and leaving the unit. Children should not be allowed to visit patients in isolation.
8. If unit does not contain toilet facilities, patient must use bedpans and urinals and have bed baths since they must be restricted to the isolation unit.
9. Good personal hygiene practices should be observed by all personnel to protect themselves against infection.
10. Disposable urinals and bedpans should be used, if available. Autoclaving is the most reliable decontamination system if nondisposable ones are used.
11. Masks should be discarded in an appropriate receptacle before the user leaves the contaminated area. They must never be lowered around the neck and then reused.
12. When caring for several patients who have the same disease, and who are hospitalized in the same nursing unit or ward, one gown may be worn when caring for this group of patients.

HANDWASHING TECHNIQUES

PURPOSE

To prevent the spread of contamination from the patient's unit to surrounding areas.

EQUIPMENT

Sink with running water
Soap/detergent in dispenser
Paper towels in container
Step-on can or waste basket lined with water proof
bag for towels

PROCEDURE

1. Turn on faucet and leave water running during washing procedure.
2. Wet hands and apply a heavy lather.
3. Lather and wash faucet, if foot or knee controls are not available.
4. Use friction, one hand upon the other.
5. Rinse.
6. Repeat steps 2, 4, and 5.
7. Turn off faucet.
8. Dry hands with paper towel. Discard in waste container.
9. Open gown by loosening tie at neck first.
10. Remove gown and place in hamper.
11. Take clean paper towel, turn on faucet and wash hands and arms and dry with paper towel.
12. If anteroom is available, cleanse hands with disinfectant towelette, remove gown in patient's room and place in hamper. Then carry out hand washing procedure in anteroom area.
    a. If gown is to be reused, cleanse hands with disinfectant towelette, remove gown and hang in patient's room and then go to anteroom and carry out handwashing technique, steps 1 through 7.

POINTS TO EMPHASIZE

1. Hands must be washed before and after patient contact even when gloves are used.
2. Any cuts or abrasions noted on hands should be reported to the doctor-or nurse before entering isolation.
3. When sinks are not available in the isolated patient's unit, hands must be disinfected with towelettes in the unit and then washed immediately under running water after leaving the unit.

MASK TECHNIQUE

PURPOSE

To prevent the spread of respiratory infection from the patient to personnel and visitors.

EQUIPMENT

Covered container of masks or box of disposable masks on table outside the patient's unit.
Paper bag for used masks in patient's room on side of linen hamper.

PROCEDURE

A. Putting on mask:
    1. Wash or disinfect hands.
    2. Take mask from container.
    3. Open mask by pulling strings.
    4. Place over nose and mouth, tie at back of head and neck.
    5. Adjust mask before going into isolated area.

B. Taking off mask:
    1. Wash or disinfect hands.
    2. Untie mask and drop in bag, taking care to touch only strings.
    3. Wash hands.

POINTS TO EMPHASIZE

1. Masks become ineffective when moist and should be discarded.
2. Masks must never be lowered around the neck and then be reused.
3. Masks should cover the nose and mouth

GOWN TECHNIQUE

PURPOSE

To prevent the spread of contamination from the patient's unit to surrounding areas.

EQUIPMENT

Gown supply in cabinet of bedside locker outside isolation area
Handwashing facilities

PROCEDURE

Putting on gown:
1. Wash hands.
2. Take gown from cabinet.
3. Put on gown and tie at neckband. Overlap back to completely cover uniform. Tie belt at waist.

Taking off gown:
1. Untie belt.
2. Wash or disinfect hands.
3. Untie neckband.
4. Slip out of gown rolling clean side over hands and forearms as it falls forward.
5. Drop in laundry hamper.
6. Wash hands.

IMPROVISED METHOD WHEN GOWNS ARE REUSED

EQUIPMENT

I.V. Standard, clothes tree or wall hooks are located within the patient's room
Gown which has been used
Handwashing or disinfecting facilities

PROCEDURE

Putting on gown:
1. Gown will be hung so that the contaminated side is out. Grasp gown by neckband and slip hands and arms into sleeves, taking care not to touch the outside of the gown.
2. Place fingers inside neckband, draw gown into place. Tie neckband.
3. Bring back edges of gown together so that inside of one side is in contact with inside of gown on other side. Lap over.
4. Grasp belt. Bring to back and tie.

PROCEDURE (Continued)

Taking off gown:
1. Untie belt. Loop in front.
2. Wash or disinfect hands. Untie strings at neck.
3. Place two fingers of right hand under cuff of left sleeve. Pull down over hand.
4. Grasp outer part of right cuff through sleeve covering left hand.
5. Slip out of gown by working hands up to shoulder seams.
6. Lift gown off shoulders touching only the neckband on the outside.
7. Fold gown and hang on hook with back seams together and contaminated side out.
8. Wash or disinfect hands.

POINTS TO EMPHASIZE

1. All personnel must know precisely how to put on gown and remove it.
2. Gown should be discarded after each use, if possible.
3. If gowns are to be reused they should be hung within the patient care unit - not in the corridor.
4. If gowns are to be reused they should be discarded always when they are wet and every 3-4 hours.

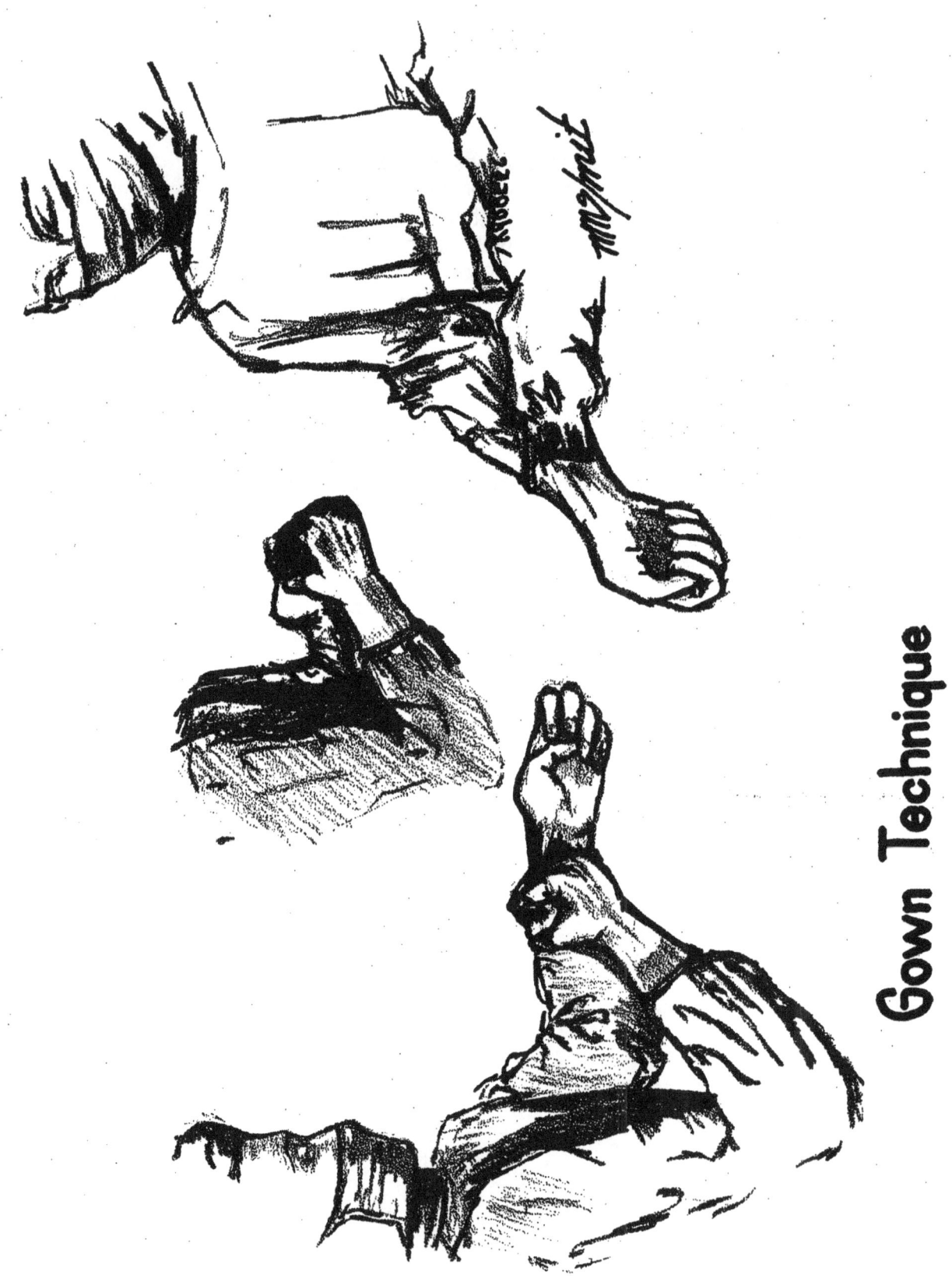

Gown Technique

CARE OF LINEN

(Double-bag Technique)

PURPOSE

To prevent the spread of contamination from the patient's unit to the surrounding area.

EQUIPMENT

Linen bags Linen hamper

PROCEDURE

1. Place hamper bag over back of chair in unit.
2. Place linen in bag as it is removed from bed.
3. If only one patient is isolated, the linen hamper for contaminated gowns may be used for bed linen.
4. Close bag tightly and then place in a second clean bag, preferably a different color, which is held by a second person or supported by a hamper outside the patient's room.
5. Close bag tightly and label "CONTAMINATED".

POINTS TO EMPHASIZE

1. Never shake out linen when removing from bed and transferring to linen hampers.
2. If hot water-soluble bag is used, it should be the inner bag.
3. Use disposable linens when available.

SERVING FOOD WITH DISPOSABLE DISHES

PURPOSE

To provide nourishment to the patient and prevent spread of contamination.

EQUIPMENT

Disposable dishes and utensils Disposable water proof bags

PROCEDURE

1. Notify kitchen to serve patient's food on disposable dishes.
2. Wash hands.
3. Obtain tray from food cart and transfer food on disposable dishes to tray in patient's room.
4. Prepare in usual manner.

AFTER MEAL

1. Enter room in usual manner bringing in disposable tray bag.
2. Pour all liquid waste food into commode in room and flush. (If no commode, empty into hopper in in utility room taking care not to contaminate utility room.)
3. Place all refuse and paper containers in the disposable bag and wrap securely. Place in clean bag that has been placed just outside the unit.
4. Wipe tray clean and replace in designated place within patient's unit.
5. Make patient comfortable and arrange unit.
6. Remove gown, gloves, and mask, if used, washing in the usual manner.
7. Carry bag containing refuse to utility room, or galley and place in garbage can for usual garbage disposal.

POINTS TO EMPHASIZE

1. Be sure all refuse is removed from the room <u>after each meal.</u>
2. Wash tray after each meal and retain in patient's unit; same tray is used for same patient at each meal.

MEDICATIONS FOR THE ISOLATED PATIENT

PURPOSE

To provide medications and prevent spread of infection.

EQUIPMENT

Disposable medicine cups
Disposable syringe and needles
Medication tray

PROCEDURE

1. Assemble medications as described.
2. Put on isolation gown and gloves (if needed).
3. Bring medications into room. (If a tray is used to carry medications it must be left outside the room.)
4. Administer medication in the usual manner. Discard cup and other disposable equipment in waste basket.
5. Remove isolation garments in the usual manner.
6. Wash hands.
7. Record medication.

POINTS TO EMPHASIZE

1. Oral medications are prepared in disposable cups.
2. For medications administered by injection, disposable syringes and needles are always used.

CARE OF EQUIPMENT

1. Discard all disposable equipment.
2. Break off tips of needles and syringes before discarding.

CARE OF BODY DISCHARGES AND EXCRETA

PURPOSE

To discard body secretion and prevent contamination.

NOSE AND THROAT DISCHARGES

EQUIPMENT

Waxed paper bag
Sputum cups Paper wipes

PROCEDURE

1. Supply each patient having nose and throat discharges with paper bag and paper wipes. If sputum is copious supply sputum cup.
2. Instruct patient to:
    a) Cover his mouth and nose with wipes held in cup like fashion whenever he coughs, sneezes or talks to people.
    b) Place used wipes directly into paper bag pinned to bed.
    c) Ask for new sputum cup when one is half full.
3. Distribute clean bags and sputum cups every 8 hours or oftener, if necessary.
4. Collect bags. Close tightly. Place in trash can for incineration.

EXCRETA

PROCEDURE

1. Each patient should have his own bedpan and urinal.
2. Use paper covers for bedpans and urinals.
3. Empty bedpans and urinals directly into bedpan flusher.
4. Press steam valve for two minutes. Use paper towel on handle of steam valve.
5. Remove bedpan/urinal and return to patient's unit.
6. Wash hands.
7. When patient is ordered out of isolation the bedpan and urinal should be sterilized by autoclaving.
8. Disposable bedpans and urinals should be used when available.

TERMINAL DISINFECTION

PURPOSE

To eliminate and destroy pathogenic organisms in the patient's unit when a patient is discharged.

PROCEDURE

1. Give patient complete bath and shampoo; give clean clothes and assign to non-isolated bed.
2. Put on gown (gloves and mask if indicated) when cleaning unit.
3. Strip unit/cubicle or room.
    a) Place all washable linen directly into "Contaminated" laundry bag/hamper.
    b) Place blanket and pillow in separate laundry bag. Mark "Special contaminated-blanket, pillow."
    c) Place all disposable materials in plastic bag outside the room in waste container.
    d) Send all utensils, instruments and thermometers to CSR for terminal sterilization. Place in plastic bag and mark appropriately.
4. Wash bed, bedside locker, chair, overbed table and entire cubicle or room with a germicical detergent solution, including walls up to six feet. Rinse. Allow to air dry.
    a. Sponge plastic mattress cover with germicidal detergent. If mattress was not protected by plastic cover and is grossly soiled with infectious discharges, burning should be considered.
5. If possible, air cubicle or room with windows open and door closed for 2-4 hours before preparing for another patient.

B. ISOLATION PROCEDURES FOR SPECIFIC COMMUNICABLE DISEASES

Type of Isolation	Diseases	Precautions
I. Strict Isolation	1. Anthrax, inhalation 2. Burns, extensive and infected 3. Diptheria 4. Eczema vaccinatum 5. Meliodosis 6. Neonatal vesicular disease 7. Plague 8. Rabies 9. Rubella and congenital Rubella syndrome 10. Smallpox 11. Staphylococcal enterocolitis 12. Staphylococcal pneumonia 13. Streptocaccal pneumonis 14. Vaccinia, generalized and progressive	1. Private Room - necessary 2. Gowns - must be worn by all persons entering room 3. Masks - must be worn by all persons entering room 4. Hands - must be washed on entering and leaving room 5. Gloves - must be worn by all persons entering room 6. Articles - must be discarded, or wrapped before being sent to CSR for disinfection or sterilization
II. Respiratory Isolation	1. Chickenpox 2. Herpes yoster 3. Measles (rubeola) 4. Meningococcal meningitis	1. Private room - necessary 2. Gowns - not necessary 3. Masks - must be worn by all persons entering room 4. Hands - must be washed on entering and leaving room 5. Gloves - not necessary

ISOLATION PROCEDURES FOR SPECIFIC COMMUNICABLE DISEASES
(Continued)

Type of Isolation	Diseases	Precautions
II. Respiratory Isolation (Continued)	5. Mumps 6. Meningocaccemia 7. Pertussis 8. Rubella 9. Tuberculosis, pulmonary-sputum-positive or suspect 10. Venezuelan equine encephalomyelitis	6. Articles - those contaminated with secretions must be disinfected
III. Protective Isolation	1. Agranulocytosis	1. Private room necessary with sterile sheets 2. Gowns - sterile - worn by all persons entering the room 3. Masks - worn by all persons entering the room 4. Hands - must be washed on entering and leaving the room 5. Gloves - must be worn by all persons having direct contact with patient 6. Articles - No special precautions 7. Visitors - limited
IV. Enteric Isolation	1. Cholera 2. Enteropathogenic E. Coli gastroenteritis 3. Hepatitis, viral (infectious or serum) 4. Salmonellosis (including typhoid fever)	1. Private room - necessary for children only 2. Gowns - must be worn by all persons having direct contact with patient 3. Masks - not necessary 4. Hands - must be washed on entering room 5. Gloves - must be worn by all persons having direct contact with patient or with artcles contaminated with fecal material

ISOLATION PROCEDURES FOR SPECIFIC COMMUNICABLE DISEASES
(Continued)

Type of Isolation	Diseases	Precautions
IV. Enteric Isolation (Continued)	5. Shigellosis	6. Articles - those contaminated with urine or feces must be disinfected or discarded
V. Wound and Skin Precautions	1. Gas gangrene 2. Impetigo 3. Staphloccal wound infections	1. Private room - desirable. 2. Gowns - worn by all persons having direct contact with patient 3. Masks - <u>Not</u> necessary except during dressing changes 4. Hands - must be washed on entering and leaving room 5. Gloves - must be worn by all persons having direct contact with infected area 6. Articles - no special precautions except for those contaminated by drainage from infected area

GLOSSARY OF MICROBIOLOGY

Contents

	Page
ACID-FAST BACTERIA .... ANAPHYLACTIC SHOCK	1
ANAPHYLAXIS ...... BACTERIOPHAGE	2
BALLISTOSPORES ...... COCCI	3
COLIFORM GROUP ...... DIPLOID NUCLEUS	4
DISINFECTANTS ...... FERMENTATION	5
FISSION .... IMHOFF TANK	6
IMMUNITY .... LYSIN	7
MANTOUX TEST ...... MYCELIUM	8
NATURAL IMMUNITY ...... PATHOLOGY	9
PERITRICHIC ...... PROTOZOA	10
PSYCHROPHILES ...... SEPTIC TANK	11
SEPTICEMIA ...... SUPPURATION	12
SYMBIOSIS....... ...... UREASE	13
VACCINE .... ZYGOTE	14

GLOSSARY OF MICROBIOLOGY

A

ACID-FAST BACTERIA - Bacteria that strongly resist decoloration with acid-alcohol after being stained with a hot dye such as carbol fuchsin. Mycobacterium tuberculosis is a typical example.

ACQUIRED IMMUNITY - Immunity that an individual obtains after a period of natural susceptibility.

ACTIVATED SLUDGE PROCESS - A method of sewage purification in which a little "ripe" sewage is added to the fresh sewage to be treated, which is then submitted to extensive aeration.

ACTIVE IMMUNITY - Immunity in which the immunizing agent is produced by the metabolism of the immunized individual.

AEROBES - Organisms that can grow in the presence of air.

AGAR - (1) A polysaccharide material extracted from sea weeds.
(2) A common term applied to a culture medium solidified with this material, such as nutrient agar.

AGGLUTINATION - The clumping together of bacteria through the action of agglutinins homologous with them.

AGGLUTININS - A kind of antibody that causes the clumping together of the corresponding antigen particles, such as bacterial bodies.

ALGAE - Thallophytic plants that carry on photosynthesis with the aid of chlorophyll or other pigment.

ALLERGY - A state of hypersensitivity to a foreign substance such as protein.

AMMONIFICATION - The formation of ammonia from organic compounds.

AMPHITRICHIC - With a tuft of flagella at each end of the cell. Resulting from cell division but not not separation of two sister cells each carrying flagella at one end. Terminal flagellation.

AMYLASE - The enzyme that hydrolyzes starch to maltose. Diastase. Ptyalin.

ANAEROBES - Organisms that cannot grow in the presence of air. ANAEROBIOSIS - Life in the absence of free oxygen.

ANAPHYLACTIC SHOCK - The response of the body to the injection of a substance to which the body is abnormally sensitive.

ANAPHYLAXIS - A state of hypersensitiveness to a foreign protein or other substance, brought about by an initial injection of the substance.

ANOREXIA - Loss of appetite.

ANTAGONISM - A relationship between species of microorganisms in which one kills or injures the other. Antibiosis.

ANTIBIOTIC - A substance produced by a living organism which will inhibit or destroy other forms of life, expecially pathogenic micro-organisms. Examples are penicillin, streptomycin, bacitracin, etc.

ANTIBODY - A substance produced by the body under the stimulus of an antigen and capable of reacting with it *in vitro*.

ANTIGEN - A substance, usually a foreign protein, that, if injected into the body, stimulates the production of an antibody such as antitoxin.

ANTISEPTIC - A chemical substance that, in the strength used, will inhibit the activities of microorganisms without killing them.

ANTITOXIN - An antibody that has the power of neutralizing the effects of the homologous toxin that served as an antigen for its production.

ASCOSPORES - Spores produced in definite numbers, usually eight, by free cell formation within a sac or ascus.

ASCUS - The spore-bearing sac of the *Ascomyeetest* ATTENUATED - Made weaker than normal, or less pathogenic.

AUTOCLAVE - An apparatus used for heating materials under steam pressure. Similar in principle to a pressure cooker.

AUTOLYSIS - Self-digestion due to the action of enzymes upon the tissues that produced them, as the over-ripening of bananas and other kinds of fruit, or the breakdown of dead bacterial cells.

AUTOTROPHIC BACTERIA - Bacterial that can live without a supply of organic matter, and can obtain energy from inorganic materials, or in some instances from sunlight.

B

BACTEREMIA - The presence of bacteria in the blood stream. Septicemia.

BACTERIOLYSIS - The disintegration of bacterial cells.

BACTERIOPHAGE - A specific virus capable of destroying living bacteria.

BALLISTOSPORES - Asexual spores formed by yeasts of the family *sporobolo-mycetaceae*. They arise on sterigmata and are shot off by a drop excretion mechanism.

BARRIERS OF INFECTION - Mechanical obstructions, such as skin and mucous membranes, that prevent pathogenic organisms from reaching a vulnerable region.

BROWNIAN MOVEMENT - The movement of visible particles by the bombardment of molecules of the suspending fluid.

BUDDING - A method of cell division in which a small area of the cell wall softens and protoplasm including a nucleus is forced out and is later cut off by constriction, thus forming a new cell.

BUTTER CULTURE - A pure culture or a definite mixture of bacterial species added to cream after pasteurization to give desire flavor and consistency to the butter made from it.

BY-PRODUCTS - Substances that remain after certain elements have been removed for use by the organism, e.g., nitrites, after oxygen has been removed from nitrates.

C

CAPSULE - A thickened slime of layer of carbohydrate material surrounding the cell wall of many species of bacteria.

CARBOHYDRASES - The group of enzymes that hydrolyze complex carbohydrates to simpler ones. The amylolytic group.

CARRIER OF DISEASE - A person or animal that harbors the orga-isms of disease without showing symptoms.

CATEGORIES - The several group names - orders, families, genera, etc. - used for classifying living things.

CELLULASE - The enzyme that hydrolyzes cellulose into cellobiose.

CHEMOSYNTHESIS - The obtaining of energy by the oxidation of inorganic substances, followed by its use for the building of organic compounds.

CHEMOTAXIS - The ability of organisms to respond to chemical stimuli by moving toward or away from the region of greatest concentration.

CHLAMYDOSPORES - Thick-walled spores formed by a rounding up of cells of a mycelium.

CHROMOGENESIS - The production of pigment.

COCCI - Bacteria that are spherical or nearly so.

COLIFORM GROUP - All aerobic and facultatively anaerobic gram negative non-spore-forming rods which ferment lactose with gas formation.

COLIPHAGE - A specific bacteriophage that is capable of destroying *Kechericha* coli.

COLONY - A visible collection of bacteria resulting from the multiplication and growth of a single individual.

COLUMELLA - A dome-shaped, non-sporeforming structure extending upward from the sporangiophore into the base of a sporangium, as in *Rhizopus*.

COMMENSALISM - A relationship between species of organisms in which one receives benefit and the other neither benefit nor harm. Metabiosis.

COMPLEMENT - A thermolabel, non-specific constituent of the normal blood of man aiding in the destruction of all kinds of bacteria.

CONDENSER - A large lens beneath the stage of a microscope, for concentrating light on the object from below.

CONIDIA - Fungus spores cut off from the tips of hyphae by constriction.

CONIDTOPHORE - A stalk arising from the vegetative mycelium and supporting sterigmata that produce one or more conidia.

CONJURATION - The union of two gamete cells in sexual reproduction.

CONSTRICTION - A method of cell division in which the cell is cut in two by a circular furrow surrounding it.

D

DARK-FIELD ILLUMINATION - A method of illuminating objects for microscopic examination whereby the object is made to appear luminous against a dark background.

DECAY - The destruction of organic materials through the action of enzymes produced by microorganisms.

DEHYDROGENASES - A group of enzymes that remove hydrogen from compounds and thus -produce the effect of oxidation.

DENITRIFICATION - The formation of free nitrogen or nitrous oxide from nitrates.

DICK TEST - A skin test to determine, whether a person is susceptible to scarlet fever.

DIFFUSE NUCLEI - Nuclei composed of chromatin material scattered throughout the cytoplasm rather than enclosed within a nuclear membrane.

DIPLOID NUCLEUS - A nucleus having a complete number of paired chromosomes for the species. See *Haploid*.

DISINFECTANTS - Chemical substances capable of killing pathogenic microorganisms.

E

EFFLUENT - Partially or completely treated sewage flowing out of any sewage treatment device.

ELECTRON MICROSCOPE - A microscope similar in principle to the compound light microscope but which uses electrons instead of light as a source of radiation.

ENDOENZYMES - Same as intracellular enzymes.

ENDOTOXINS - Toxins that remain within the cells that produce them and do not stimulate the production of corresponding antitoxins.

ENVIRONMENT - The composite of all conditions surrounding an organism.

ENZYME - A biological catalyst.

EPIDEMIOLOGY - The science of tracing the sources from which diseases spread.

ETIOLOGY - The science of causes, e.g., causes of disease.

EXCRETIONS - Substances that have become so changed in composition through metabolism that they are no longer useful to the organism that produced them and are cast off, e.g., carbon dioxide.

EXOENZYMES - Same as extracellular enzymes.

EXOTOXINS - Toxins that diffuse from the cells that produce them into the surrounding medium. They are antigenic and stimulate the formation of antitoxins.

EXTRACELLULAR ENZYMES - Enzymes that diffuse out of the cells that formed them. Exoenzymes.

F

FACULTATIVELY ANAEROBIC - Organisms that can grow in either the presence or absence of air.

FACULTATIVELY PARASITIC - Organisms that can live either as parasites or as saprophytes.

FALSE BRANCHING - A kind of branching of filaments in which the cells do not branch, but the branch of the filament is held to the main filament by a common sheath surrounding both.

FERMENTATION - A process carried on by microorganisms whereby organic materials, usually carbohydrates, are decomposed with the formation of acids and sometimes carbon dioxide and alcohol.

FISSION - A method of cell division by constriction in which two daughter cells of equal size are formed.

FLAGELLA - Slender protoplasmic strands that extend from the cell and serve as organs of locomotion.

FUNGI IMPERFECTI - A heterogeneous group of fungi that have no sexual stage. Apparently most of them are degenerate. *Ascomycetes.*

FUNGUS - A thallophytic plant that lacks chlorophyll and is of filamentous structure.

G

GAMETES - Two haploid cells that unite in sexual reproduction.

GENOTYPE - The sum total of the determinants controlling the reaction range of an individual or a cell.

GROWTH -   (1) Increase in size of an individual.
(2) Increase in numbers of microorganisms.
(3) A visible mass of microorganisms formed by reproduction and enlargement.

H

HANGING DROP - A drop of liquid suspended for study from the under side of a cover glass mounted on a slide with a depression in the surface.

HAPLOID NUCLEUS - A nucleus having a complete number of single chromosomes for the species. See *Diploid.*

HUMUS - Organic matter decomposed to such an extent that its original structure is no longer recognizable.

HYDROLASES - Enzymes that bring about chemical change by the addition of water that goes into chemical union with the substance acted upon.

HYPERSENSITIVITY - An abnormally high degree of sensitiveness to foreign substances such as proteins.

HYPERTROPHY - The abnormal multiplication of cells resulting in the formation of nodules, tumors, etc.

HYPHAE - Branches of a fungus mycelium.

I

IMHOFF TANK - A specially constructed septic tank having a flow chamber above and a sludge chamber below.

IMMUNITY - The ability of an animal or plant to resist disease even when the pathogenic organisms or their products reach a vulnerable region.

IMPRESSED VARIATION - A kind of variation brought about by some recognizably unfavorable condition.

INFLAMMATION - A morbid condition characterized by swelling, redness, and pain, usually in a localized region.

INFLUENT - Sewage, treated or partially treated, flowing into any sewage treatment device.

INOCULUM - Material containing microorganisms and used for the inoculation of media or hosts.

INTERMITTENT STERILIZATION - A sterilization process involving the heating of the material to a temperature of 80-100 C for a time up to an hour on each of three successive days. Fractional sterilization. Tyndallization.

INTERMOLECULAR RESPIRATION - A form of respiration in which oxygen is taken from one kind of molecule and used to oxidize another.

INTRACELLULAR ENZYMES - Enzymes that remain within the cells that produced them. Endoenzymes.

INTRAMOLECULAR RESPIRATION - A form of respiration in which there is a rearrangement of atoms within the molecule resulting in a release of energy.

INVOLUTION FORMS - Cells of microorganisms large in size and of unusual form. Generally considered abnormal.

IRON BACTERIA - Bacteria that contain ferric hydroxide in the stalk or the sheath.

IRRITABILITY - The capacity of an organism for response to change in the environment.

L

LENS - A piece of glass or other transparent substance used for magnifying or reducing the apparent size of objects.

LIPOLYTIC ENZYMES - Enzymes that hydrolyze fats into fatty acids and glycerol.

LOPHOTRICHIC - With flagella in a tuft at one end of the cell. Terminal flagellation.

LYOPHILIZE - To dry a protein, usually from the frozen state, in such a way so it is still soluble. As applied to microorganisms it involves the freezing and drying of the organisms so that many of the cells will remain viable for long periods of time.

LYSIN - An enzyme or other substance that breaks down or dissolves organic substances.

M

MANTOUX TEST - A tuberculin test in which the tuberculin is injected intradermally.

MASS MORPHOLOGY - The morphology of bacterial groups, colonies, etc., as contrasted with individual cells.

MECHANISM OF INFECTION - The means by which microorganisms produce disease.

MESOPHILES - Bacteria that grow best at moderate temperatures, having an optimum of 25°C to 45°C.

METABIOSIS - Same as commensalism.

METABOLISM - Any chemical change brought about by a living thing in its use of food.

MICROAEROPHILIC - Organisms that require free oxygen of less concentration than that found in the atmosphere.

MICROMANIPULATOR - A complicated piece of apparatus used for fine dissection under the microscope, or for single cell isolation.

MICRON - A unit of measurement having a value of 0.001 of a millimeter.

MICROORGANISMS - Forms of life that are microscopic in size, or nearly so.

MICROPHILES - Bacteria having a narrow temperature range for growth.

MILLIMICRON - 0.001 micron or 0.000001 mm. A unit of measurement often used in designating the size of virus particles.

MITOSIS - Division of a cell with a diploid nucleus in which all of the chromosomes divide, resulting in two diploid daughter cells.

MOLD - A saprophytic fungus that is of simple filamentous structure.

MONOTRICHIC - With a flagellum occurring at one end of the cell. Terminal flagellation.

MORBIDITY - The frequency of occurrence of cases of a disease.

MORPHOLOGY - That branch of biological science that deals with qualities that appear to the eye - size, form, color, etc.

MORTALITY - The percentage of deaths among those afflicted with a disease.

MUTATION - A change from some parental character occurring in the offspring. More permanent than variation.

MYCELIUM - The branching, thread-like structure that makes up the vegetative body of a fungus.

N

NATURAL IMMUNITY - Immunity that an individual possesses by virtue of its race or species. Immunity present from the beginning of life of the individual.

NECROSIS - The death of tissues.

NITRATE REDUCTION - The formation of nitrites or ammonia from nitrates.

NITRIFICATION - The formation of nitric acid or nitrates from ammonia.

NITROGEN FIXATION - The formation of nitrogen compounds from free nitrogen.

NON-SYMBIOTIC NITROGEN FIXATION - Fixation of nitrogen by organisms living independently, as *Azotobacter* and *Clostridium.*

NOSEPIECE - The portion of a microscope into which the objectives are screwed.

O

OBJECTIVE - The system of lenses in a compound microscope that is used next to the object to be studied.

OCULAR - The combination of lenses at the top of a compound microscope. Also called an eyepiece.

OIDIA - Thin walled spores formed by the separation of undifferentiated cells of a mycelium.

OPSONINS - Antibodies which make bacteria more readily ingested by phagocytes.

OSMOSIS - The tendency of fluids to pass through a membrane that separates two portions of different concentration.

P

PARASITES - Organisms that obtain their food from the living substance of other organisms.

PASSIVE IMMUNITY - Immunity in which the immunized individual does not produce its own immunizing agent but receives it from one with active immunity.

PASTEURIZATION - Heating at a temperature that will kill most objectionable microorganisms, excepting sporeforming bacteria and thermophiles.

PATHOGENICITY - The ability to produce disease.

PATHOGENS - Organisms that cause disease in other forms of life.

PATHOLOGY - A study of the abnormal conditions that occur in the tissues as a result of disease.

PERITRICHIC - With flagella distributed all over the cell body. Lateral flagellation.

PHAGOCYTES - Leucocytes or other living cells that have the power of ingesting bacteria.

PHENOL COEFFICIENT - The killing strength of a disinfectant, relative to that of phenol.

PHOTOGENESIS - The production of light. Phosphorescence.

PHOTOSYNTHESIS - The formation of carbohydrates from simpler food materials, using light as a source of energy.

PHYSIOLOGY - That branch of biological science which deals with the functions and activities of living things - nutrition, growth, reproduction, irritability, etc.

PLAQUES - Clear zones in streaks of bacterial growth resulting from the lysis of bacteria by bacteriophage.

PLANE OF DIVISION - The direction in which a cleavage furrow divides a cell.

PLASMODESMID - A protoplasmic strand extending from one bacterial cell to another.

PLASMOLYSIS - The shrinkage of cell contents through the withdrawal of water by osmotic action.

PLEOMORPHISM - Exhibiting several forms or shapes. Polymorphism.

PLEUROPNEUMONIA GROUP - Microorganisms that grow in cell-free culture media with the development of polymorphic structures as rings, globules, filaments, and minute reproductive bodies.

POLYMORPHISM - Exhibiting several forms or shapes. Pleomorphism.

PORTALS OF INFECTION - Openings through which pathogenic organisms pass into the body of the host.

POST-FISSION MOVEMENTS - Movements of cells following fission, whereby the two adjacent cells are finally separated.

PRECIPITINS - A kind of antibody that forms a precipitate with an antigen that was previously in solution.

PROCESSING - Preliminary treatment, canning, and sterilization of foods. The term is often used for a single one of these operations such as sterilization.

PROTEOLYSIS - The destruction of proteins by enzymes.

PROTEOLYTIC ENZYMES - Enzymes that hydrolyze proteins and related compounds.

PROTOZOA - Unicellular members of the animal kingdom.

PSYCHROPHILES - Bacteria that grow best at relatively low temperatures, having an optimum of 15°C to 20°C.

PUTREFACTION - The chemical decomposition of proteins and related compounds, usually with the production of disagreeable odors.

R

R-COLONIES - Colonies that have a rough surface, although belonging to a species that usually produces smooth colonies.

REFLECTED LIGHT - Light that strikes the surface of an object being studied with a microscope and is reflected back into the lens.

RENNIN - The enzyme that changes the soluble casein of milk into the solid paracasein in the presence of calcium.

RESOLVING POWER - The ability of a lens to reveal fine detail. It is measured in terms of the least distance between two points at which they can be identified as two rather than as a single blurred object.

RESPIRATION - Any chemical reaction whereby energy is released for life processes.

RICKETTSIAE - Microorganisms that are obligate intracellular parasites or that are dependent directly on living cells. They are not ultramicroscopic but are adapted to intra-cellular life in arthropod tissue.

ROPY MILK - Milk that is viscid because of the presence of capsule forming bacteria such as *Alcaligenee visconsus.*

S

SAPROPHYTES - Organisms that use non-living organic matter for food.

SCHICK TEST - A skin test to determine whether a person is susceptible to diphtheria. Similar to the Dick test for scarlet fever.

S-COLONIES - Colonies that have a smooth surface, although belonging to a species that may produce rough-surfaced colonies.

SECONDARY INVADERS - Saprophytic organisms that invade the body of a host in the wake of a pathogenic species.

SECRETIONS - Substances that serve a useful purpose to the organisms that produce them, e.g., enzymes.

SEPTATE MYCELIUM - A mycelium subdivided into cells by cross-walls or septa.

SEPTIC TANK - A deep vat or chamber used for the anaerobic treatment of sewage.

SEPTICEMIA - The presence of bacteria in the blood stream. Bacteremia.

SEWERAGE - The system employed for the handling of sewage.

SLIME LAYER - A carbohydrate layer surrounding all bacterial cells which, if it becomes extensive, is called a capsule.

SLUDGE - The mass of solids remaining after a sewage treating process is completed or wet sewage solids which have been deposited by sedimentation.

SOURCES OF INFECTION - Places from which disease-producing organisms were acquired by the host.

SPECIFICITY - The limitation of a species of microorganism to one species of host, or to at least a small number.

SPONTANEOUS COMBUSTION - Ignition of material by heat generated through its oxidation.

SPONTANEOUS GENERATION - The origin of living things from nonliving materials.

SPORANGIA - Sacs in which fungus spores are formed. SPORANGIOPHORE - A stalk that produces a sporangium.

SPORANGIUM - A sac that contains spores, usually numerous and indefinite in number.

SPORE - (1) A simple reproductive body of a lower plant, capable of growing directly into a new plant.
(2) Among bacteria, a thick-walled resistant cell.

STERIGMATA - Tiny stalks that produce spores at their tips, as in *Aspergillus, Penicillium,* and mushrooms.

STERILIZATION - Killing microorganisms, usually by means of heat.

STOCK CULTURE - Cultures of microorganisms kept as a reserve for future use.

STREAK CULTURES - Cultures made by applying the organisms with a loop or other instrument to the surface of a medium, usually agar slanted in a test tube.

STRICT PARASITES - Organisms that require a living host.

STRINGY MILK - Milk that contains tough stringy clots as it is drawn from an inflamed udder.

SULFUR BACTERIA - Bacteria that use sulfur or hydrogen sulfide for food and oxidize it. Some forms store granules of sulfur in their cells.

SUPPURATION - The formation of pus.

SYMBIOSIS - A relationship between species of organisms whereby each receives some form of benefit.

SYMBIOTIC NITROGEN FIXATION - Nitrogen fixation by bacteria living symbiotically with higher plants.

SYMPTOMS - Functional disturbances brought about by diseased conditions.

SYNERGISM - The ability of two or more species of organisms to bring about chemical changes that neither can bring about alone.

T

THERMODURIC BACTERIA - Organisms capable of withstanding high temperatures.

THERMOGENESIS - Heat production by microorganisms.

THERMOLABILE - Destroyed by a temperature below the boiling point of water.

THERMOPHILES - Bacteria that grow best at relative high temperatures, having an optimum of 55C or higher.

THERMOSTABLE - Resistant to heat at the boiling point of water or thereabout.

TOXEMIA - A condition characterized by toxins in the blood.

TOXINS - Poisonous substances of complex nitrogenous composition produced by bacteria and some higher organisms.

TOXOID - A detoxified toxin that remains antigenic and can be used to confer active immunity.

TRANSMITTED LIGHT - Light that passes through the object that is being studied with a microscope.

TRICKLING FILTER - A sewage purification plant in which the sewage is sprayed onto a layer of crushed rock or similar material to provide an extensive surface or aeration.

TUBERCULIN TEST - A test to determine whether a person or animal has been infected with *Mycobacterium tuberculosis*.

U

ULTRAMICROSCOPE - A microscope that reveals very minute objects by the use of light that strikes them obliquely and is reflected into the objective.

UREASE - The enzyme that hydrolyzes urea into ammonium carbonate.

V

VACCINE - Anything which, if injected into the body, causes it to develop active immunity.

VARIATION - The departure of the offspring from the parent with respect to some character. Usually more temporary than mutation.

VECTORS OF DISEASE - Insects or other forms of animal life that transfer pathogenic organisms from host to host.

VEHICLE OF INFECTION - Food or water containing pathogenic microorganisms.

VIRULENCE - In bacteriology, the ability to produce disease.

VIRUSES - Etiological agents of disease, typically of small size, most being capable of passing filters that retain bacteria, increasing only in the presence of living cells, and giving rise to new strains by mutation, not arising spontaneously.

W

WIDAL TEST - The agglutination test for typhoid fever.

WINOGRADSKY TEST - A soil test for fertility by determining its suitability for growing *Azotobacter*.

Y

YEAST - A kind of fungus which has been reduced to a more or less unicellular state by loss of mycelium.

Z

ZYGOSPORE - The zygote of certain kinds of fungi and algae, e.g. *Rhizopus, Mucur* and *Spirogyra*.

ZYGOTE - A diploid cell formed by the union of two haploid gamete cells in sexual reproduction.

www.ingramcontent.com/pod-product-compliance
Lightning Source LLC
Chambersburg PA
CBHW081818300426
44116CB00014B/2406